Practical Magick for the Penny Pinching Witch

Copyright © 2012 by Carol Roper-Moyer
All rights reserved. No part of this book may be used or reproduced in any manner whatsoever, including internet usage, without written permission from the author.
ISBN: 1481221159
ISBN-13: 978-1481221153

This book is dedicated to:

My Mommy and Daddy, thank you for raising me to be the strong and independent woman that I am. May you always rest in peace; I love and miss you both!

My amazing children, Shayna and Dawson, for always loving me even when I am spazzing out over nothing.

My amazing hubby, Marcus, for always supporting me in all of my crazy endeavors and for loving me like no other man ever has or will.

My sisters, Sophie and Robyn, just because I love you and cannot imagine my life without you.

My brothers, REB and Lance, you are both the closest thing to real brothers I will ever have and I cannot imagine my life without you both being in it.

My Witchy sisters, Stephie and Terri, for always being there to help a Witch out when she needs it and for always supporting me.

Without all of you this book would have never been possible. I love you all more than you will ever know!

Contents

Introduction 1
Altar 4
Bath Salts 10
Candles 14
Flowers and Resins 24
Herbs 27
Incense 33
Inks 45
Kitchen Gadgets 49
Oils 55
Ritual Sand Drawings 61
Ritual Soaps 64
Tinctures 68
Tools of a Witch 72
    Athame 74
    Pentacle 75
    Wand 75
    Censer 76
    Chalice 76
    Broom 77
    Boline 78
    Cauldron 78
    Bell 79
    Book of Shadows 79
Sabbats 81
    Yule 81
    Imbolc 82
    Ostara 82
    Beltane 82
    Midsummer/Litha 83
    Lammas/Lughsnasadh 83

- Mabon 83
- Samhain 83
- Correspondences 84
  - Colors 85
  - Colors by Magickal Property 86
  - Flowers 89
  - Flowers by Magickal Property 91
  - Gems and Stones 95
  - Gems and Stones by Magickal Property 103
  - Herbs 110
  - Herbs by Magickal Property........................... 120
  - Magickal Days 130
  - Magickal Days by Magickal Property 133
  - Resins... 146
  - Resins by Magickal Property.......................... 148
  - Tincturing Herbs 151
  - Tincturing Herbs by Magickal Property 153
  - Woods... 155
  - Woods by Magickal Property.......................... 160
- Sacred Texts... 166
  - The 13 Principles of Wiccan Belief................. 167
  - The Witches' Creed.. 170
  - Rede of the Wiccae or Wiccan Credo 173
  - The Law of Power 176
  - Charge of the God.. 178
  - Charge of the Goddess 181

Introduction

With the economy in the shape it has been in for the past several years, there are many Witches who have had to give up their regular rituals because they simply cannot afford to purchase the supplies they need. I understand your pain and I have done the leg work and the research to be sure that you, the modern Witch, are able to continue practicing the Craft without breaking the bank.

Within the covers of this book you will find ways that you can buy all of your supplies at your local grocery store, health food store, drug store or at supercenter stores. There is no need to spend hundreds of dollars on herbs at specialty stores when you can buy the same things much cheaper buy shopping in the spice aisle at your local grocery store or health food store. The same goes for candles. Many dollar stores carry candles and they usually cost around $1 for three votive candles and you can get them in a wide array of colors. Incense can also be bought at a novelty store for about $1 for 10 sticks or you can use herbs sprinkled over a tea light candle instead which can save you tons of money in the long run. Resins are bit more difficult to deal with, but in the resin section of this book I will discuss ways of getting around having to use them.

I want all of you to be able to go about your daily ritualistic lives without breaking the bank or you feeling like you just cannot do the rituals you need to because you think you cannot afford the items that are called for in your spells. After reading this book, I believe that you will be able to go about your practice of the Craft, confident that you can do this easily and more manageably.

The correspondences and information that you will find in this book have come out of my head after years of trial and error, years of research, years of reading countless books and websites and from years of meeting with and chatting with other Witches. It is very possible that you will see some of the same information here in other books but that is because we are all learning. Witchcraft is not something we can all go to college for to become experts on. We all have to learn in any way that we possibly can.

With that being said, I hope you enjoy the book and I hope that you are able to save yourself a lot of money and headaches by using what I am going to present to you.

Brightest Blessings to you and yours!

Altar

An altar should be the center of your magickal practice. It should not be viewed as a shrine, per say, but an area where you will work your rituals. This is where you will work with your herbs, your incense, your magickal tools, and so forth. The altar, simply put, is any flat surface at which you have ample space to work with any tools you will need for your rituals.

Not every witch is able to have an altar. You may not have the space for it, especially if you live in a small apartment or dorm room or you may have small children or pets that will constantly be coming in contact with the altar. For those who are not able to have a full scale altar, you can always envision your altar in your mind. This will actually force you to concentrate harder on the work at hand. However, if you are lucky enough to have an altar, there is no need to have a whole slew of items strung out across your altar making it unfunctionable. I like to be able to work on my altar, and I do not like having to worry about knocking things over, or having to constantly move things around, so I keep my altar items to a minimum. On my altar, I have three candles, one for the Lord, one for the Lady, and one to represent fire. I have a bowl of water, a bowl of dirt, a statue of my deity, a wand, an athame, my Book of Shadows, and a flat centerpiece that is a pentacle. Some of the items that are on my altar are gifts. My Lord candle is gold, my Lady candle is silver and my fire candle is red. The bowls that I use for water and dirt I purchased from a retail store that sold dishes as separates and I purchased two bowls that were to be used for nothing more than holding water and dirt. In the beginning, I used a piece of paper with my deity's name written on it. Later I used a photo of a statue of my deity, and now I have a small statue of my deity. My wand is made of willow, Weeping Willow to be exact. I have a friend that has a huge Weeping Willow tree, and I asked him for permission to remove several branches. Once I gained his permission, I then asked permission of the tree, the Lord and Lady and then removed nine evenly sized branches. I took them home, consecrated them as magickal tools, opened a circle, and proceeded to braid three branches together, then another three branches together, then the last three branches together, then I braided the three braids together and wrapped consecrated white ribbon around the two ends to keep it from coming apart. Thus I have my own wand, which cost me nothing more than my time and the few pennies that I spent on the ribbon to hold the braids together. I started out using a letter opener for an athame. There are many states that will not allow people to have knives of any kind shipped to them. If this is the case, you may never find that special athame you want. So in the mean time, find an office supply store and buy a letter opener. General kitchen knives are not generally acceptable because the blade should have a double edge, and most kitchen knives only have one sharp edge. However, you can use that until you are able to get a letter open if necessary. Remember, it is the intent that matters most. My centerpiece started out as a laminated piece of paper with a pentacle drawn on it. I laminated it so that it would not get damaged if I spilled water, dirt or melted wax on it. Later on, I was given a brass pentacle that I now use for the centerpiece of my altar.

    I am sure by now you are wondering what I use for the altar itself. Well, lucky for me, I have a crafty husband who works well with power tools. I found, at a local lumber store, a precut, round, pine table top that is about three feet in diameter. I used a wood burning tool to burn in various signs and emblems that I wanted to be a permanent part of my altar, then I used polyurethane to seal the wood. I then used wooden table legs, three of them, and made my altar three feet tall. All in all, I think I may have put about $50 into the table. But that beautiful altar of mine came after years of finding whatever I could use as an altar. I have used cinderblocks, my kitchen table, milk crates with boards on them and I have even used the floor with a rectangle drawn with consecrated chalk or consecrated tape marking the boundaries of the altar. The possibilities are only as endless as your imagination. As witches, we are crafty people by nature and sometimes that craftiness has to come out just so you can have an altar. If you do not have hundreds of dollars to spend on purchasing an altar or making one, do not fret, the Lord and Lady are not going to strike you down for making an altar in the middle of your living room floor with masking tape. It is all about intent.

There are other things that you may wish to have on your altar, though they are not mandatory items. Incense is great for spell work because it adds smell and visual smoke for the element of air. Cakes are used as offerings and can either be something that you have baked yourself, which is my preference as it adds even more intent to the spell work at hand, or they can be individually wrapped snack cakes that you have bought from your local grocery store that you have consecrated as ritual tools. A chalice can either be a fancy glass or goblet that you have purchased or it can be a coffee cup or cup from your current collection of everyday cups that you have consecrated as a ritual tool. Brooms can either be purchased from your local dollar store, many have straw brooms, or many craft stores will have small brooms that look like the ones many witches use, just remember it is all about intent. Cauldrons are also great especially if you plan on having to burn anything. These are typically cast iron, and you can burn anything in them. Just remember that cauldrons can be heavy and quite expensive and they also must have something protective under them if you are going to be burning anything in them as they are great conductors of heat, and I do not want you burning down your home! If you cannot acquire a cauldron, you can use a metal pot that you have consecrated as a magickal took. Just remember that if you use a metal pot that was once used for cooking in, chances are good that once you light a fire in it cooking in that pot will not be possible anymore. Bells are typically used to banish negativity, invoke deities, and prepare sacred space as in house blessings. Typically, one ring means the beginning of the spell or ritual. Three rings of the bell signifies a pause or for clearing an item of its negativity. Four rings of the bell will seal the magickal act. Five rings of the bell are used to invoke the quarter energies. Seven or twenty-one rings are use to call on the dead and nine rings of the bell will invoke deity.

What you need to remember is that your altar is a focal point of energy that is positive and it is a culmination of your energy and that of Spirit. Where the altar is matters less than how you use it. The shape of the altar does not matter, it is personal choice. Having more than one altar is not necessary, but there is nothing wrong with it either. You should not use your altar or place any ritual or magickal tools on it until you have consecrated the altar as a magickal tool.

~ 10 ~

Bath Salts

Ritual bath salts are an amazing substitution for herbal baths. How many times have you taken an herbal bath only to get out covered in wet leaves and spend the next half an hour cleaning the tub because there are wet leaves stuck all over the inside of the tub? I have done that once, and only once. Sure, you can put the herbs in a sachet, but for me, I enjoy the art of making bath salts, and being an earth sign, I really enjoy the art of making the bath salts and then using them. Another thing I love about bath salts is how pretty they look in their jars, and I love giving them as gifts (non-ritually charged unless asked for) to my friends.

Making bath salts is ridiculously simple. All you need is a glass jar, Epsom salts, baking soda, and table salt. I use glass canning jars which you can purchase at most grocery stores; Epsom salts can typically be found in the beauty aisle of most pharmacies and table salt, well that stuff is really cheap at the grocery store. If I am making the salts for a friend I will get a piece of cloth in either a color they like or one that complements the salt if it is ritually charged and I will place it between the top of the jar and the lid and I will then tie a ribbon of the same color around the outside of the lid once the lid has been screwed on. The piece of cloth is not a necessity, but it does help with keeping moisture out if the salt is going to be stored in a bathroom where there is typically a higher rate of moisture in the air.

Now then, on to the fun part – making the bath salts. In a large bowl, preferably one that is non-metallic, mix 3 parts of Epsom salts, 2 parts of baking soda, and 1 part of table salt. Mix these thoroughly with your hands. If you are using this salt for ritual purposes, be sure to empower the mixture with your intent. Once the mixture is well blended you can add color if you want. This is done through a simple process of using common everyday food coloring that is found in the baking aisle of your local grocery store. Start out with a few drops and mix with a spoon until the entire mixture is colored. If you want a darker color, add more food coloring, if you want a lighter color, add less food coloring. If you need to mix colors to make blended colors such as purple, mix these together in a spoon first and then add them to the salt mixture. If you add the colors separately you will end up with multicolored salt rather than a blended color such as the purple tint you were hoping for. You are now ready to add your essential oils. Add your essential oils one drop at a time and one ingredient at a time. Typically speaking, you should not add more than about ten total drops of essential oil per half cup of bath salt. This is the most time consuming part of the whole process. Mix with a spoon until all of the particles are moist. As you are mixing, if you are planning on using this as a ritual bath salt, be sure to visualize your intent throughout the entire process, so that you can fully empower your bath salt. Once you have mixed your oils into the salt it is either ready to use or to be stored.

Before you fill your tub with water, be sure that you have wiped it down with baking soda and rinsed it out very well. Visualize any negativity that may be in the tub from previous use being wiped away and washed down the drain. When you are ready to add the salt to your bath, you can add anywhere from a couple tablespoons to a quarter of a cup of the salt mixture to your bath water. Stir the salts around in the tub in a clockwise motion with your hand. Feel the energies that are in the salts mix with the energy of the water. Then, when you are ready to get in the tub, slide in and allow yourself to soak in the power of the water and the salts that you have mixed in the water. When you are finished with your ritual bath, be sure to wipe the tub down with baking soda and rinse it out again. Again, be sure to visualize any energy that may be left be hind in the tub being wiped away then rinsed down the drain.

Candles

Candles can represent a multitude of things in a witch's life. They can represent the Lord and Lady on an altar, mark the four quarters in a magickal circle, represent the element of fire on the altar or they can represent a specific person, place or thing in a spell. Candles can also be a magickal timing device and they can be a magickal working in and of themselves. Typically, the size and shape of the candle do not matter, at least not in my opinion. I have read many books, visited many websites, and talked with many witches that will state a candle has to be a specific color, shape, and size according to the spell you are working. I have found this to be untrue in my own practices. The intent is what matters most, not the physical appearance of your candle. One thing to keep in mind on size and shape is your working area and the length of time you will need to burn the candle. If you have an area that is large and can support large shaped candles, then shape may not be an issue. If, however, you have a small confined space, you will likely want to choose a candle that is small and in its own container. If you need a candle to burn for an extended length of time, 7-day jar candles work great because they last for a great length of time. I have found that 7-day jar candles are great because once you are finished with a particular spell; you can release the charge you placed on the candle and put it away to use again for a different spell. This not only saves you money, but it will allow you to use a candle for multiple spells.

    On your altar, if you have one, you should have a candle that represents the Lord and a separate candle to represent the Lady. These candles can either be colored specific by having a gold or yellow candle for the Lord and a silver candle for the Lady. White can be used for both, as white can be used to represent any color of candle. If you choose to mark the four quarters of your circle with candles, you can either use the appropriate colors for those quarters, or again, you can use white.

The candle that represents fire on your altar should be red; however, it is not always easy to find a red, unscented candle. If you are unable to locate a candle of this nature, you can again simply use a white candle. If you are using a candle to represent a specific person, place or thing, you can always use a white pillar or taper candle, and carve the persons name, the name of a place or thing into the candle. If you wish to use the candle as a timing device, I recommend using a pillar candle and carving notches into the sides of the candle.

Candles do have color properties that will correspond to the magickal workings you are performing, however, something that is great to remember, no matter what you are doing, a white candle can ALWAYS be substituted for any color candle a spell will call for. Also, I have found it best to use candles that are unscented, as scented candles will also have properties of their own as well. In the back of the book you will find a list of the color correspondences for candles. The list is not meant to be complete on all of the correspondences to candle color; these are just the ones that I have found through my years of study of the Craft and through my own practices. You may find that certain colors do different things for you in your practices and that is perfectly fine.

After years of asking every witch I have ever come across, the consensus seems to be that a candle should

NEVER be blown out if it is being used for magickal purposes. Candles should always be snuffed out because blowing them out is actually using your life force to extinguish another. You can either purchase a candle snuffer, or you can make one yourself using some aluminum foil and a cheap knitting needle, or a metal spoon or fork and some tape. I used a knitting needle and electrical tape. Simply make a bell shape out of the aluminum foil with a long enough point on the end to wrap around the knitting needle or other utensil, then use tape to secure the aluminum foil to the handle. These work great and can be thrown away if they get crushed or if you prefer to not reuse them. Of course you will want to keep whatever you attached the aluminum foil to, but the foil itself can be discharged and recycled when you recycle the rest of your aluminum.

I have had many witches ask me if it is better to make our candles rather than buying them. My answer to this is it really does not matter, but I enjoy making candles, so when I have the time, I would rather make the candles that I need instead of purchasing them. The problem with making candles is you have to worry about flashpoints, additives, preservatives, and so on. It can become quite a pain and quite expensive if you are going to make a lot of candles on a regular basis. However, if you are going to make just a few, I suggest going to a local thrift store, or a dollar store and purchase white candles, then purchase some candle wicking, and go from there. If you purchase white candles and melt them down slowly, the additives and preservatives are already there to prevent flash fires from occurring. This can also be much cheaper than purchasing paraffin or beeswax, along with all of the additives, the preservatives, and the colorants to make your own candles completely from scratch.

So, for the sake of saving money and being crafty, I am going to discuss how you can melt down used or new white candles and create your own ritually charged candles. I love going to the thrift stores and finding candles that are used. Often times you can pick up an almost whole six inch pillar candle for less than a dollar. You can also use tea light candles; these can usually be purchased in bags of twenty or more for less than $10. When I burn candles in my home for their scent, I always save the jars they come in. I know these jars can handle the intense heat of the candle so I do not have to worry about buying a pretty jar, then pouring scalding hot melted wax into it only to have it shatter under the intense heat of the wax (I have actually done that, so PLEASE, take my advice, use only jars that are meant to have high heat substances in them.) You can also use canning jars, as these are strong enough to withstand the heat of the melted wax. If you are going to use left over candles jars, I advise buying a candle warmer, which you can purchase for about $10. This will warm the entire jar, melting any wax that may be left over so that you can pour it out, but you have to be quick because the wax will solidify quickly. If you do not want to mess with cleaning used jars out, you can typically pick up a case of canning jars for about $15.

    Back to the candle making process. First you will need to measure your candle wick to be sure that it will hang to the bottom of the jar. You can do this by wrapping one end around a pencil and set the pencil on the mouth of the jar. Keep wrapping the wick around the pencil until it either just touches the bottom of the jar or is just shy of touching the bottom of the jar. Secure the wick with some tape so it does not come unwound. You will then need to set up a double boiler process if you are not going to purchase a candle warmer. A double boiler is where you fill a pot with enough water that it will cover half of the jar without overflowing the pot. You will then put the jar into the boiling water, and add your wax until it is all melted and you have the desired amount in the jar. For the purposes of ease, I will be giving direction on using a candle warmer, since it is safer and much easier. Candle warmers can generally be purchased for about $10 where ever you buy candles. When using the candle warmer, I set it on the counter in my kitchen, and plug it in. I will then remove the tea light candles from their bases and remove the wicks. I then charge each candle and empower it with the intent that I plan on using it for. I then place a few of the tea light candles into a jar and set it on the candle warmer and I walk away. I will go back every hour or so and check on the wax, as it melts down I will add another tea light to the jar, keeping track of the level of the wax in comparison to the height of the jar since I do not want the wax to run over the top of the jar. Once all of the wax has melted and I am satisfied with the amount of wax that is in the jar, I will then use old crayons to color the candle. I simply break them up and add them to the melted wax. These will melt and will color the wax. Just remember, that the color will be a couple shades lighter as the wax hardens, so depending on the color density you want, you will need to adjust your crayon amounts. The great thing about making candles with the warmer is you can let the wax set to see the final color. If you want it darker, you add more crayons. If you want it lighter you will have to melt it back down, pour some of the wax out and then add more white candles to it. This takes more time, but allows you to get the exact color you desire. Once you have the color you desire, it is now time to add your herbs or oils. If you are using herbs, chances are there will not be much of a scent when you burn the candle. If you are going more for scent, then you will need to use essential oils. Use enough oils so that you can smell the aroma coming off of the wax. As you add the oils or herbs, you will need to stir in a clockwise motion while visualizing the intent and goals you have for the candle. Once you are happy with the candle being thoroughly mixed, it is now time to set the wick in the candle. You will have to dip the wick into the candle and let it dry several times before it is heavy enough to sink to the bottom of the jar. Once it is heavy enough to sink to the bottom of the jar unplug the candle warmer. Wait a few minutes for the wax to begin to cool off and then insert your wick making sure that you have it in the center of the jar and that it hangs straight. An abnormality in the way the wick is positioned can cause abnormal burning of the candle at a later time. Leave the candle alone until the jar is no longer warm to the touch. It is then ready to use whenever you need it.

    Many witches prefer to use taper candles in their spell work. So in this section I will list the steps you will to take to make taper candles. Again, I will be using the candle warmer, since it is safer. You will need a jar that will be a little bit taller than the desired length of your tapered candle. This completely depends on you, the ritual time needed for the burning candle and the space you have available. I like shorter candles for ritual purposes, and if I use taper candles for the altar candles that represent the lord and lady I prefer them to be a little longer so I do not have to make them as often. Choose what you like the best. I do not typically add herbs or oils to the wax when making taper candles. If I am going to use oils, I will simply anoint the candle with the oil when I am ready to use it. I use the exact same method for making taper candles as I do for making jar candles, as outlined above, with the exception of the wick and adding oils and herbs. You can add oils and herbs if you wish, I just choose not to. I melt the candle wax in the jar and then add crayons for coloring. When I am ready to start dipping the wick, I do so a few times to get some weight on the wick by allowing the wick to dry between dippings. This will give the wick the weight that it will need to go all the way to the bottom of the jar. After you are able to get the wick to go to the bottom of the jar, you will need to let the wax dry between each dipping. This will make the process go much faster. As you dip the candle each time, be sure to visualize your intent and magickal goals. Continue dipping and drying until you achieve the thickness desired for your taper candle. Once this is achieved you will need to gently roll your candle on a piece of wax paper to remove irregularities that occur during the dipping process. This needs to be done shortly after the candle has started to harden but before it has set up completely. Once it has started to dry, you will then cut off the cone shape on the bottom, be sure to do this before the candle sets up completely as this will make it easier to remove the cone. You will then need to let the candle hang upside down until it has dried completely. Once it has dried completely, dip the candle three more times, allowing it to dry between dippings and hang to dry one last time. Once the candle has cooled completely, it is now ready for you to use.

Flowers and Resins

Flowers can be a bit of a different story when it comes to convenience of grabbing a few buds. You cannot just readily run to the corner store and pick up a bottle of dandelions. However, many grocery stores have a floral department where you can purchase various flowers. Or you can go to the local florist and see if they have what you need for your spell. One great thing to remember about flowers is that you can always use Rose as a substitution for ANY flower. If you have a "green thumb" you may wish to plant some flowers that you can use in your spell work. Obviously you have to wait for the growth process to occur, but in the end you will have flowers that you planted, cared for and charged with your own energy. This has never been an option for me because I am not inclined to taking care of plants, they always die because I either overwater them or forget to water them. Many witches will decide they would rather not mess with finding flowers for a spell and they will instead substitute an herb that has the same magickal properties as the spell they are working on and use that instead. This works great for witches like me who are allergic to every single wind pollinated plant that exists as well as most other flowering plants. So, if you decide to substitute an herb for a flower, then you would just simply find the herb that has the same magickal properties as the flower you would have been using. In the back of the book there is a list of common flowers that are used in magickal spells. This list is obviously not inclusive, but it is meant to be a starting ground for your research on using flowers in your spell work. One very important thing to remember is that many plants are toxic to animals as well and you need to keep this in mind if you have pets. Through my research I have found 397 plants that are toxic to cats, 392 plants that are toxic to dogs and 284 plants that are toxic to horses! This is vital information to have if you are going to grow your own plants if you have pets that could potentially come in contact with the plants. While, as

Witches, I believe that growing your own plants will add your own magickal signature to your plant which will add power to your spell, the last thing I want to happen is for your beloved furry friend to get sick or pass away because they decided to eat one of the plants that you decided to grow. In the plant and flower correspondence charts, I have marked the toxic plants accordingly based on my research.

    Resins are a completely different issue and I rarely use them because of their cost and availability. Resins generally have to be purchased from a new age store or from a website. These can get a little expensive, so one thing to remember is that frankincense can be used as a substitute for any resin that a spell calls for. What many witches will do, and what I do, is find an herb that has the same properties as the resin a spell calls for and use that instead. Whether or not you choose to use resins is completely up to you since it is the intent that matters most.

Herbs

All plants, woods, oils, resins and gums have their own unique energy signature. You will need to know which herbs have what properties, but you will also need to know how to blend them with other herbs to strengthen their properties to better aid your working. You will also need to know how best to obtain the herbs, oils, or resins that you may need.

There are three ways of obtaining the herbs that you will be using for your spell work: collection, growing your own and purchasing the herbs that you will need. For many, collecting the herbs in nature may be easier said than done which can also apply to the growing of the herbs. For witches like me who are allergic to many things in the woods, and who could not grow a plant of rosemary to save my soul, purchasing is pretty much my only option.

    If you are going to collect the herbs, you would simply walk wooded areas around your home, if you have them, or you could climb mountains, walk beaches or travel through deserts to find your herbs. If you are going to collect your herbs from their natural environment, you need to remember a few things before you traipse off into the woods, with cutting shears in hand. Collect ONLY WHAT YOU NEED! Be sure that you attune yourself with the plant before you take anything from it. Never take more than a quarter of the total plant. If you are collecting the roots, then obviously you have to take the whole plant, so be sure to take only the one plant and leave the others around it untouched. Never collect your plants or roots after a heavy rain or dew, until the sun has had a chance to dry the plant out so that mold does not form while the plant is drying out in your home. Also, be sure to choose the collection site of your plants with great care. You never want to collect plants that are near a highway, stagnant or polluted water, or factories. Anytime you take something from a plant, be sure to leave something behind. This can be as simply as a coin, a few drops of milk, or something you have crafted as a means of showing your gratitude to the plant and Mother Earth for providing the plant. This shows that you are thankful for what the plant has given you and you are willing to give back to the Earth for what you have been given. Chances are though that many of the herbs you are you going to use cannot be found right outside your back door. This leads to growing the herbs yourself.

Growing herbs can be very rewarding, as you plant the seeds, watch the seedlings sprout and then watch the plant grow into something that will readily make herbs available to you. However, herb gardens can require a lot of work, and can be quite consuming of space, and if you do not have a massive room in which you can grow hundreds of types of herbs, you may have to stick with either gathering them or purchasing them. If you have decided to grow your own herbs, be sure to guard them magickally by placing a small quartz crystal in the soil. You can also wear jade while you are watering them or tending to them.

For convenience sake, it is often much easier, and faster, to just purchase the herbs that you will need on a regular basis. Just because an herb is purchased does not lessen its magickal value. Just be sure that you are purchasing what you are in fact wanting to purchase. There will be places that will say they are selling you one herb, when in fact it is really something else. It is sad to say that there are places out there that do this, but it is true. This is especially true if you are ordering through the mail or from the internet. Ask around and see if there are any reputable suppliers of herbs in your area, or on the internet. Also, be sure to avoid any packaged herbs that are mostly stems, have discoloration, or are moldy. If an herb is supposed to be heavily scented and it in fact has a light scent, chances are it is not the herb you are wanting, or it could be mixed with something else or it could just be old. Also please remember that suppliers can only sell what they can get from the growers.

    Dealing with herbs can be a daunting and terrifying task for some witches because there are so many different herbs and each herb has so many different correspondences it can be difficult to figure out which one would be the best for the spell or magickal working you are preparing for. Another bothersome feat is figuring out where in the world you are going to get some Mugwort or Dragon's Blood. Some herbs can be very hard to find and when you do find them they are very expensive. Some herbs, are poisonous and ingesting them or breathing smoke produced by them can be very dangerous, even deadly. Finally, some herbs just plain out stink. So, there are ways around the troubling and sometimes mind-boggling issue of using herbs in spell work. My aim is to have you completely prepared and calm about the use of herbs by the time you finish this chapter. I plan to have you successfully using herbs that have all come from your local grocery store! Yes, that's right; many of the herbs that your spells will call for can be purchased at your local grocery store! It will be these herbs, and only these herbs that I will list in this book. If you are already headed to the grocery store to purchase your weekly round of groceries, then there is no reason that you should have to order a bunch of herbs from some internet website, pay outrageous prices, then have to pay outrageous shipping prices and risk getting something that is not what you ordered to begin with. You are already going to be at the grocery store, so go ahead and take a trip down the spice aisle and you will be amazed at all of the magickal herbs you can pick up.

If you decide to purchase your herbs from the grocery store, keep in mind they need to be kept in a cool, dark place, and tightly sealed. This will prolong the life of your herbs greatly. I have herbs that I purchased years ago, that when opened, are still as strong in smell as they were the first time I opened the bottle. Another thing to keep in mind, when using herbs, is understand your body. NEVER use an herb that you are allergic to. Also, pay attention to your senses, if an herb is giving you a bad vibe from the smell, or it makes you ill, stop using it immediately. If you become ill from coming in contact with an herb, contact a physician right away.

There are literally hundreds of herbs that grow on our planet, and at the end of the book I will have a list of the most common herbs that are used in witchcraft and they can be purchased at the local grocery store. Obviously, this list of herbs will not be inclusive, as it will only be the herbs that are available at grocery stores. Whenever in doubt, do not use an herb until you have done plenty of research to be sure that it is not toxic in anyway, not just generally, but that it is not toxic to you or anyone around you because they are allergic. Another tip to remember is that rosemary is a substitute for any herb. So, as long as you have no issues with rosemary, then your herbal issues will always be cured because you can replace any herb with rosemary.

Incense

Incense is something that has become somewhat of a staple to witches across the globe. It can be burned to promote ritual consciousness, which is a state of mind that is very necessary to rouse and direct the personal energy that you have within you into your magickal workings. Incense can be burned before your ritual workings to purify the area that you will be working in of any negativity. This chapter will be dedicated to incense, making it and the various types of incense that can be used. I will cover making combustible, non-combustible, incense papers, how to use these types of incense, and then a correspondence table will be at the end of the book for the different types of incense and their magickal properties.

Incense, just like herbs, has its own magickal properties that will attract certain energies to the magickal workings at hand. During rituals, incense will take on a magickal transformation. The energies that were once trapped within the unburned incense are now let out and will then mix with the environment of the witch and the magickal area. This will allow the properties of the incense to send out the energies to aid in the obtainment of the goal at hand.

If you have incense in your home, and you wish to use it to freshen up the smell of your house, do not use incense that is meant for magickal purposes. You can make incense for this specific purpose. Using your magickal incense to freshen up your house will do nothing more than waste the energy of the incense.

Making incense is actually fairly easy. Not only can it save you some money, but it will add your personal intent to the incense, along with the natural energies of the incense. Incense is actually comprised of leaves, flowers, roots, bark, resins, gums and oils. You can also add semiprecious stones to your incense to add a boost of the stones energy to the incense, thus making it more powerful. One thing you do need to remember when preparing your own incense is that many plants will smell very different when they are being smoldered. Many sweet scents can turn very sour very quickly. So, it may be a good idea to test a few out before committing them to becoming your next favorite incense. You can do this by dropping a small portion of the herb onto a hot block of charcoal and let it smolder. Then you can decide if the scent is pleasing or not. There is nothing worse than putting the time and energy into an incense only to find out that it is not a smell you can live with. Having pungent smelling incense can be very distracting during your rituals, so it is best to test and be sure before you end up with scattered energy because an incense that smelled good before it was burned now smells like rotting flesh. It may be a good idea, when you get ready to set out on your adventure of making your own incense, to have a small notebook handy so that you can keep track of herbs that you have smoldered and their smells, and any other effects they may have on your psychically, physiologically, or emotionally. This will also allow you to build knowledge, through experience, of herbs, their smells and your reactions to them.

    There are two forms of incense that are used: non-combustible and combustible. The biggest difference between the two is that combustible incense contains saltpeter (potassium nitrate) which is used to aid in the burning of the incense. This is typically found in your formed incense such as sticks, cones, and blocks. Non-combustible incense can just be sprinkled onto a block of glowing charcoal. It does not matter which one you use. The power is in the properties of the herbs that are used and the scent they put off. I prefer stick incense, but for me that is a matter of convenience. I find it much easier to just buy the incense that I need rather than spending the time on making it. I have a busy life, and that life does not always allow for me to make the crafty things for ritual that I would like to. Either way, remember that incense can be either combustible or non-combustible. It does not matter. What matters is the smell, the energy and what works best for you.

    Non-combustible incense can easily be made. Gather all of your ingredients before hand. Then ground each ingredient into a fine powder. This can be done in a mortar and pestle, in an herb grinder or in a blender. What matters is that the ingredient is reduced to a powder. Some resins will not reduce to a powder easily, so these will take some time and some experimentation to see which methods work the best for you. When all is ready, fix your mind on the goal of the magick you will be working. In a large, preferably wooden or ceramic bowl (any medium can be used, but it is best to use something non-metallic), mix the powdered gum or resin ingredients together with your fingers. Feel the energy from within you moving through your body into your arms, down to your hands and out of your fingers into the powder. This is what makes your handmade incense better and more effective – it has your energy intermixed into it. Next, you will mix the powdered leaves, barks, flowers or roots into the bowl. Again, mix together with your fingers and feel the energy from your body move into the mixture. Visualize your goal as you mix the ingredients together. Now add any liquids to the mix. Usually, a few drops will be all that you need. And mix again, using the method of empowerment listed above. Once everything is thoroughly mixed and you are satisfied with the amount of energy and intent that you have put into the mix, you can add any powdered gems to the mix. If you are going to add stones to the mix, simply smash the stone with a hammer to crush it then use your mortar and pestle or other grinding device to grind the stone into a fine powder. Add no more than a very tiny pinch to the mixture and follow the guidelines above. Once this is done, you are then ready to smolder your incense or you can store it in a tightly capped jar. Be sure to label the jar with what is inside, adding the herbs, stones, oils, resins and any other objects to the label, along with the use of the incense, the name of the incense and the date that it was made.

To use non-combustible incense, you will need a self-igniting charcoal block and you will need to place it in a fire safe and high heat safe dish such as a censer. Once you light the charcoal, the saltpeter stops crackling and the charcoal is glowing, you simply sprinkle about a half of a teaspoon of your incense onto the charcoal block. This will allow the incense that you have worked hard to make smolder and produce its fragrant smoke. As the smoke begins to thin out, add a little more to the block. As the incense burns, there will be ash that will form; you do not need to knock this off unless it starts to smell badly. If you add too much to begin with you will likely smother the charcoal which will cause it to go out. Also remember that incense that is mostly resins or gums will burn much longer than those that are most made of wood and leaves.

Combustible incense, which comes typically in the shape of cones, blocks and sticks, can be a complex manufacturing process, but there are many that feel it is well worth it in the end. The basic ingredient of all shaped incense is gum tragacanth. This can be purchased at some herbal stores or at some drug stores. It can be a little on the expensive side, but a little bit will go a long way. If you are unable to find gum tragacanth, you can try using gum arabic. You will need to make what is called tragacanth glue, which is done by placing a teaspoon of the ground gum tragacanth in a glass of warm water. Mix thoroughly until all particles are evenly dispersed throughout the water. Gum tragacanth has enormous absorption properties, with one ounce being able to absorb up to one gallon of water within a week.

Let the tragacanth absorb the water until it becomes a thick and bitter smelling paste. If you are making stick incense, the consistency will need to be a bit thinner, whereas for cones or block incense the consistency will need to be thicker. When the tragacanth glue is made, cover it with a wet cloth, and set it aside. It will continue to thicken as it sits, so keep an eye on it. If it becomes too thick for what you want to do, then simply add some more water and stir well. You will next need to make up your incense base. The following pages will show the ingredients and procedure for making your incense base. The incense base has the following ingredients:

- ✯ 6 parts ground charcoal (NOT self-igniting)
- ✯ 1 part benzoin
- ✯ 2 parts sandalwood
- ✯ 1 part orris root (to set in the scent)
- ✯ 6 drops essential oil (for best results, use the oil form of one of the herbs that you have used)
- ✯ 2-4 parts of mixed and empowered incense
- ✯ Saltpeter (potassium nitrate)

Mix the first four ingredients until they are all well blended. Add the drops of essential oil and mix again with your hands. The main goal here is to create a powdered mixture that has a fine texture and is empowered with the energy and intent of the working you will be using it for. You can run the mixture through a grinder if you wish. Then you will add two to four parts of the completed and empowered incense mixture that you made before and then combine everything well with your hands. The whole time you are mixing, be sure that you are visualizing your goal. Once you get everything mixed, you will then need to weigh the mixture so that you can add ten percent of the weight in saltpeter. You can generally purchase a food scale at health food stores or you can purchase a postal scale at many office supply stores. These types of scales allow you to weight items in grams and ounces and would be a wise investment if you are going to make a lot of incense. So, if you have made ten ounces of mixture, you will need to add one ounce of saltpeter. Mix this until the white powder is completely blended. If you add too much saltpeter, then the mixture will burn too fast, similarly, if you add too little, it may not burn at all so be sure that you measure several times just to be sure. Next you will add the tragacanth glue. Do this one teaspoon at a time, mixing with your hands, in a large bowl. Continue mixing until all ingredients are wet. For cone incense, the mixture will need to be very stiff. However, if the mixture is too thick, it will not properly form and it will take an eternity to dry out. The mixture should easily hold its shape. Using a piece of wax paper, mold the incense into the basic cone shape that you have probably purchased before. This shape is necessary for the incense to burn properly, so do your best to not deviate from the shape. Once you have the incense shaped, then you can set it in a warm, dark, and dry place for the next week to give it time to dry completely. Once the incense has dried completely, you are then ready to light it and use it in your rituals.

If you are going to make block incense, make a 1/3 inch thick square of the stiff dough like mixture that you used for the cone incense on a piece of wax paper. Then cut the mixture with a knife, much like you would cut small brownies, then separate them slightly and allow them to dry completely.

If you are planning on making stick incense, remember that your mixture will need to be a little thinner. Add more of the tragacanth clue to the mixed incense until the mixture is wet but still rather thick. The biggest issue in making stick incense is finding the proper sticks to use. The type of stick incense that you buy in stores is typically made with very thin bamboo splints which are not readily available. You can try making your own bamboo splints, or you can use broom straws. Once you decide what type of stick you are going to use, you will then dip the stick into the mixture and let them sit upright. This will take several dippings in order to get the right thickness, and this is also the hardest part of the whole process of making stick incense. Once the sticks have accumulated the proper amount of mixture, stick them into a block of clay or some other substance so that they will stand upright through the drying process. Be sure when you mix your ingredients that you have twice as much powdered wood as you have resins. If the amount of resins is too high, then mixture is not going to burn. Whatever the resin is that you have used, it should never be more than one third of the final mixture.

When you are using combustible incense, you simply need to light the incense, wait until the tip is glowing and then blow it out. You can set it in your censer or in any other incense burner.

Incense papers are another form of combustible incense that I absolutely LOVE. Instead of using charcoal or gum tragacanth, you will use tinctures, saltpeter and paper for the basic ingredients of this amazing variation of incense. See the section on tinctures for ways of making them. Gather some white blotter paper and cut it into strips that are about an inch wide and about six inches long. Add about one and a half teaspoons of saltpeter to an eight ounce glass of warm water and stir it very well until the saltpeter has dissolved completely. Place the strips of paper into the solution of water and saltpeter until the papers are all completely saturated. Remove the strips from the solution and hang them up to dry. The biggest problem you are going to have with paper incense is getting past the natural smell of the burning paper. The best things to use to overcome this issue are tinctures that are made with resins and gums. Essential oils just do not seem to do the trick here. Once you have chosen the tincture that you want to use, you will need to empower it with your magickal goal. Once you have empowered the tincture you will need to then put a few drops of the tincture on a dried strip that you prepared earlier in the saltpeter solution. As you add the drops of tincture to the strips, smear them around to cover the paper. Keep doing this until the paper is completely coated on one side. Hang the strip up to dry. Once the strip is dry, place it in a labeled air tight container until you need to use them.

To use the incense papers, you will light them, just as you do stick or cone incense, then blow the paper out so that it will smolder, rather than just go poof and it is gone. I have found if you bunch the bottom end up a bit you can stick it in a censer full of salt and it will stand in the salt and smolder down just like a stick of incense. The trick to incense papers smoldering properly is to be sure there is air all around it, which is why standing it in salt works so well. You can use unscented incense papers as a form of charcoal block if you wish. You simply need to light the incense paper, as you would for allowing it to smolder on its own, then you will sprinkle a small amount of herbal incense onto the paper and the herbal incense will smolder as it does on a charcoal block.

An important thing to remember is that you do not have to make elaborate mixtures for your incense. You can use one ingredient if you like, simply grind up the ingredient really well, empower it, and smolder it. It is that simple. Simply find an ingredient that has the magickal property that complements your magickal goal, and use that as your incense.

Inks

Magickal ink has been used in rituals by witches for many years. Many witches today, however, will rob themselves of complete involvement in a ritual by scribbling something on a piece of scrap paper with a pen they found in a desk drawer. Why do this when you can make your own ink?

Making your own ink can be as simple as going out in the woods and finding a fallen twig and charring the end of it and then using that as a writing utensil. If you are going to use this method, you will need to make a new char-pen for each ritual that you perform. You simply burn the end of the twig until it becomes charcoal (not ash) and then you let it cool and use that to write with. While you are burning the end of the twig, visualize your intent, and continue visualizing your intent while the twig cools off. Once the twig is cool, you can then use it.

You can also make liquid magickal inks, and these will require the use of a quill or a dip pen. Dip pens can usually be found at any stationary store and some office supply stores. Which ever you decide to use, you will need to practice with the quill or dip pen until you are used to the way it functions.

The easiest way to make magickal ink is by using lampblack. It is a long process, but it is well worth it in the end as you have made the ink yourself, saved yourself some money and you have added your own personal power to the ink while you are making it. When using lampblack as the method for making your ink all you need is a candle of appropriate color (white if for general purposes, or if you do not have the proper color candle), a metal spoon, a small piece of card stock or cardboard to scrape the spoon, a small bowl, gum arabic and some distilled water. You may also need something to hold the spoon with if it starts to get hot.

Light the candle, and hold the bottom side of the spoon in the flame until the bottom of spoon is covered with soot. This typically takes about 30-60 seconds depending on the size of the spoon, size of the flame, and how close you hold the spoon to the flame. Once the bottom of the spoon is covered in soot, hold the spoon over the bowl and use the card stock or cardboard to scrape the soot into the bowl. Be careful not to breathe too heavily, as this stuff is almost weightless and will happily fly everywhere if you let it. Also, be sure to do this somewhere where it will not get on your carpet, as it will stain fabric. Repeat this process about sixty times, which will take you anywhere from half an hour to an hour. While you are doing this, if you are making this ink for a specific goal, visualize that goal while you are burning the spoon, and scraping the soot into the bowl. If the spoon gets hot, use a pot holder so that you do not burn your hands. Once you are finished gathering the lampblack (soot), you will need to add, one drop at a time, some hot distilled water. Stop adding water before you think you should. Use your finger to mix the soot and water until the soot has completely dissolved. Lampblack will float on the top of the water, so it will take some effort to get it to dissolve completely. Once the lampblack is dissolved completely, and you have rich dark colored water, add some powdered gum arabic to the mix and again stir with your finger until the gum arabic has dissolved. Add enough gum arabic to make the ink have the same consistency has commercial produced ink. After you have completed the ink, you can store it in a jar and use it as needed.

When I make a magickal ink, as I use it I will write out my spell, or draw an image of my goal on a piece of paper that is appropriate to the work at hand. As I write or draw, I will visualize the letters or drawing glowing with the power from the color of the paper and from the energy within me that is being transferred into the ink as I write or draw. Sometimes I will anoint the paper that I am using with oils that also correspond to the work at hand. If you make inks that are of specific intent, be sure to label them before you put them away. If the ink sits for a while between uses, it may be necessary to shake them gently to get the ingredients mixed back together again. If you have to do this, while you are shaking the ink, be sure to visualize your intent, as this will help to empower the ink even further.

Kitchen Gadgets

Believe it or not there are several gadgets that you may already have in your kitchen that you can use for magickal purposes. Coffee makers, blenders, and crock pots can all be used to make things like magickal teas, infusions, decoctions, washes and incense. Even better, these items will likely save you a lot of time when preparing your magickal needs. To save space and money, I typically use my everyday gadgets for magickal needs when I need to. I just simply clean the item very well, visualizing the energies that are already in the gadget being washed away. I then consecrate the item as a ritual tool and I am off the magickal world of using kitchen gadgets to make my magickal supplies.

Coffee makers can save a witch a lot of time when it comes to making teas, infusions, decoctions and washes. All you have to do is add your herbs to the coffee filter, add the water, press the start button, say your necessary chant for whatever you are making, and presto, in the length of time it takes to brew a pot of coffee, you have created a perfectly, magickal tea, infusion, decoction or wash that could have otherwise taken you hours or even days to prepare. If you are going to be preparing anything that has a poisonous herb in it, I would highly suggest that you purchase a coffee pot that will be used strictly for anything that is not fit for human consumption. Many dollar stores carry coffee pots for around $5 or $10 dollars, and these will be a valuable addition to your magickal tools because then you will not have to worry about mixing poisonous herbs in the same pot you brew your daily cup of joe in. I have two separate coffee pots that I use for magickal brews. I bought them both at a thrift store, and I think I may have paid $5 for the pair. These two pots are consecrated as magickal tools and get used for nothing else but magickal brewing. I put a label on one of them reminding me that it is for poisonous materials so that I never forget which one is which. After any magickal brewing, you should always clean the coffee maker with bleach water. This not only cleans the coffee maker, but it also cleans away any of the magickal residues left behind. Also be sure to wash the pot itself with bleach water. If you are brewing anything using a root or bark material, be sure to tie the root up in a coffee filter, let it run through the brewing cycle place the root, still encased in the coffee filter, in the pot of freshly brewed liquid, leave it on the warmer plate, and let it sit for at least thirty minutes.

Many witches prefer to make their own incense, which can be fun and will aid in the magickal intent that is laid into the incense itself. Making incense does not have to be difficult, nor time consuming, not with the aid of a blender. The best part: no more buying charcoal discs to burn powdered incense on, again saving you money. All you need is your herbs, some sawdust, which many lumber yards will give you for free, and a blender. The first thing you need to do is put your herbs in the blender. Only use a couple tablespoons, this will help prevent the motor on the blender from overheating. While the herbs are swirling around in the blender, concentrate on that swirling motion, imagining your intent. Once the herbs are reduced to a fine powder, remove them and put in a couple tablespoons of sawdust. Again, you will concentrate on the swirling motion while imagining your intent. Once the sawdust is reduced to a fine powder, throw in your freshly powdered herbs, and blend for a couple seconds, again concentrating on your intent. Once your herbs and wood powder are blended, you are off to burning freshly made, magickally charged incense. If you are powdering gums or resins, you will need to add a few drops of rubbing alcohol to the mixture to make sure that the blades do not get all gummed up. The alcohol will evaporate and will not leave any vibrational energy behind, so you do not have to worry about it messing with the herbs or resins that you are using. The blender will become very handy for any mixing, grinding, or powdering job that you will have to do. This will replace the mortar and pestle, and not only will the blender out perform the mortar and pestle, but it will save you a lot of time. Just as you do with the coffee pot, be sure to clean the blender between each magickal preparation. You can clean the blender by putting in a tablespoon or two of rubbing alcohol and a cup of water and letting the blender run for a few seconds. This will not only remove any oils or extracts left behind but it will also remove any magickal energy that was left behind by the herbs and sawdust. I have a separate blender that I use for magickal workings that has been consecrated as a magickal tool. I picked this blender up at a dollar store and I think I may have paid $10 for it. I use it for making incense, potpourri, and powders.

Crock pots (slow cookers) and electric potpourri pots can be amazing money savers when it comes to making your own oils. You will be astonished at the money you can save by making your own oils. The more traditional ways of making oils can take weeks, even months for the oils to reach their proper consistency. Now, I do not know about you, but I do not have the time or the space to have a bunch of bottles of oils lying around steeping. If I need a particular type of oil, I need it yesterday, and I do not have the time or the patience to wait weeks or months for an oil to be ready to use. This is where the crock pot or potpourri cooker comes in handy. Preparing oils in your crock pot or potpourri pot is actually pretty simple. You use one part of whatever herbal mixture you need to one part vegetable oil, stir it well and cover. If you are working with fresh herbs, rather than dried herbs, you will need to bruise the herbs first by placing them in a plastic bag and pounding them a few times with the side of your hand. I have sometimes used a meat pounder for this as well. Place the cooker on the lowest heat setting possible to prevent scorching of the herbs. Check the oil every six to eight hours for scent. If the scent is not strong enough, add another helping of herbs, still well and recover. Each time you check the scent, be sure to wipe any moisture off of the lid and be sure to not remove the lid any more often than necessary. Generally, twelve to fourteen hours will produce excellent oils that are not gummy or sticky. For best results, I recommend using a light and unscented vegetable oil or fruit oil. Glycerin-based oils will eventually turn rancid. If you are going to make larger quantities of oils, I prefer jojoba oil, however, if you are just making up a small amount and it will be used fairly quickly, regular cooking oil is fine. This process of making your own oils will take several hours, even up to several days depending on how strong you want the scent of the oil, and I have found that saying a chant of intent at the time I add the herbs and oil together, and each time I stir or check on the oil, that it will charge the oil while it is cooking. The next section on oils will going into more specific details on how to make your oils.

Oils

Having been a practitioner of the Craft since the early nineties I have had many new witches ask me about making their own oils since the cost of essential oils can be very, very, VERY expensive, depending on the type of oil you are purchasing. However, making oils, while very rewarding, is a long and difficult process.

To make true essential oils requires expensive and extensive equipment such as fractioning columns, condensers, and other equipment that can be very expensive. Making essential oils also requires a very large amount of fresh plant materials to make a substantial amount of an essential oil and I do not know of many people who have a few hundred pounds of fresh eucalyptus lying around their homes. Making essential oils is an exact science, so if you leave out one step, or something is not done just right, the oil may come out smelling wrong or it will be of a substandard quality. However, for those that are completely determined to make their own oils, I have used a method that does work, though it will not produce the same high quality essential oils that you can purchase from a reputable supplier.

As stated above, you are going to need a lot of plant material, so for me, when I do decide to take on the week long task of making oil, I will use herbs rather than flowers as these are much easier to get in bulk. The only problem with this is they are typically dried herbs, so it can take much longer to get even minuscule results. I have found that many local grocery stores are starting to carry more and more fresh herbs, which makes oil making a little easier. So, check your local grocery stores, health food stores, organic food stores, and if they do not have any fresh herbs, ask around, someone may know of where you can get them. Or you can grow your own, which is not an option for me because I have a cat that eats every plant in front of him and I could not grow a plant if my soul depended on it.

Once you have found your herbs, you will need just a few other things. You will need a crock pot/slow cooker and some oil that has a pale color and a very mild scent. I have found that jojoba oil works best as it is more of a liquid wax than an oil so it does not turn rancid, but this can be a little difficult to find and can be a little on the expensive side without doing some research. You can however use safflower oil, olive oil or sesame oil and have decent results. Once you have your oils and your herbs, the following steps should lead you to a decent essential oil that you can use without having to spend a ton of money.

Gather your herbs. If you have fresh herbs you will need to bruise them by pounding them in the palm of your hand. I have also used a ritual blade to lightly score the plants to allow the natural oils an easy release. Fill your crock pot with about 6 cups of oils and set the temperature to low. If you set it on high you will risk scorching the oil thus ruining the entire batch. I typically place about 8 ounces of herbs into the crock pot for each steeping. Place the lid on the crock pot and visualize your intent for as long as you feel necessary. Then leave the crock pot to simmer for at least eight hours. After about eight hours, go back and check on the herbs. Using a wooden spoon, stir the herbs lightly and again spend some time visualizing your intent. Wipe any condensation from the inside of the lid and recover the pot. Allow the herbs to steep for another eight hours. At the end of this second eight hour period, remove the lid and strain your oil. Be careful not to burn yourself as the oil will be very hot. Once you have removed all of the herbs from the oil, place a fresh eight ounces of herbs into the crock pot, again visualizing your intent. Again, wipe all condensation from the inside of the lid and cover the pot again. You will continue to do this process until the oil has a rich fragrance that you are happy with. This can take several days depending on the herbs that you are using. I have had herbs that have taken upwards of a couple of weeks before the oil had a decent fragrance. So you will simply have to trust your nose and trust your inner self as you let the oil steep. Once you are sure that the oil has reached its proper scent, you will then strain the oil one last time and you will need to store it in a dark, glass bottle (for best results) and you will need to store it in a cool dry place. Only open the oils as you use them. If they do turn rancid, take them outside and discard them in the earth. If kept properly, the oils should keep for several months. I have had a few that only lasted a month or so, and others that have kept for a year or better, it really just depends on the herbs and the oil that you use. In my experience, jojoba seems to last the longest, so if you are going to make oils in quantity, I would highly suggest spending the extra money on jojoba oils. If at all possible, whatever oil you use, try to find out if there were any pesticides used on the plants that make up your oil. Your best option would be to purchase your oils from an organic or health food store. If you have trouble finding dark colored jars or bottles, I have found that making a bag out of black fabric works just as well to keep all of the light out of the jar. If you are going to make a bag, be sure that you empower it with the intent of the oil that will be residing inside the bag as the color of the bag could alter the oil. I have also used construction paper in a color that matches the intent of the oil. Construction paper is very thick and pretty cheap and it will block out all of the light if you cover the jar completely.

    I have had many people ask me about mixing oils. This is an easy task to do, much easier in fact, than making the oils. You will simply need to gather the oils you will need to combine, along with a clean and sterilized glass jar and about one eighth of a cup of oil. Again, jojoba is the best, but you can use safflower, sunflower, almond, olive or grape seed oils if you do not have jojoba. Use an eyedropper and add the essential oils in the proportions recommended in the recipe you are making. Once you have added the essential oils, swirl, do not stir, the mixture in a clockwise motion, visualizing your intent and ultimate goal. Be sure to store the oil in a cool, dark place away from any moisture.

When it comes time to use your oils, whether they are ones that you have made yourself, or ones that you have purchased remember that you must always use them while visualizing your goals and empower them as you use them. Many witches will rub the oils onto their ritual candles. By doing this, the oil mixes with the color, and thus you have boosted your ritual powers. Be sure to use an oil and color that have the same magickal properties, so they do not accidentally cancel each other out. Oils can also be used to anoint the body. Care must be taken, however, if you are going to place any oil on your body as some herbs can cause severe irritation to the skin, and some herbs are just down right deadly. So be sure that you know the properties of the oils that you plan to place in contact with your skin. You can also add several drops of oil to a ritual bath, slip into the bath and inhale the fragrance, but again, make sure that you know if the oil has a poisonous herb in it. You can also use the oils to anoint any talismans or sachets that you have made. You can use a corresponding oil to rub a stone, crystal or gem to boost the energy of the stone.

Ritual Sand Drawings

For those have studied Native American history you may be familiar with the common Navajo healing rituals of using sand paintings. The Navajo medicine man or shaman will take the colored sand into their receptive hands and they would allow the sand to seep from a closed fist while they drew the necessary images onto the ground. This is a type of image magick where you physically create an image of your magickal goal and then use the image you created with the colored sand as part of the ritual you are working. These images are not permanent, so new sand paintings are made each time a ritual is performed.

Some practice may be needed before hand so that you can get the hang of drawing with sand that is falling from your hand. If you let the sand fall too quickly, there will be clumps of sand, which could distort the image. So take some time and learn the right technique that will work best for you. You will be glad you did when you can sit back in your ritual and look at your artwork with pride rather than looking at it in disgust.

You can find colored sand at many craft stores. However, for the sake of saving money, I am going to tell you how to make your own colored "sand". All you need is common food coloring, found in the baking section of your local grocery store and some common everyday table salt.

Decide what colors you will need and how many. Then gather the proper number of bowls as you will need a separate bowl for each color. I have found that using the food color that is in the squeezable jars work the best because they allow you to add the coloring one drop at a time. Once you have your salt poured out into your bowls, typically about one cup, you are now ready to add the food coloring. Simply add the food coloring one drop at a time and stir the salt very well to make sure that it all gets coated. It typically takes about ten drops of food coloring to get a nice rich color for one cup of salt. Once you are happy with the color, you are ready to move on to your ritual space and use the newly colored salt as your ritual sand. If you need the color white, simply leave the salt uncolored.

If you like the results of the ritual sands, it may be a good idea to make notes of how much sand you used and how much food coloring you used to get the desired color. Be sure to list the separate colors that you used and how much of each color you used to achieve the shade. This will save you a lot of time in the future. For some added assistance, I have added a food coloring mixing chart for you below. I have made this following chart by experimenting on my own. So try the colors first before you commit to them in your ritual sand.

Color Desired	Number of drops used of each primary color			
	Red	Blue	Green	Yellow
Black	3	3	3	3
Brown	3		3	
Indigo	3	6		
Orange	6			18

For the colors blue, dark green, green, light blue, and red you will just have to add the colors until you get the desired result. For gold I use yellow and for pink I use small amounts of red.

Ritual Soaps

Many of the soaps you purchase today have tons of chemicals in them and they have horrible fragrances that are not even close to what they should smell like. You can purchase ritual soaps from some new age shops, but in my opinion, it is better to make them yourself. Not only will you ultimately save money, but you will add your personal power to the soap which means that you do not have to worry about the energies of someone else tainting your soap.

You will need a melt and pour soap base, which can be purchased at some higher end craft stores, or you can purchase it online. I typically use a clear melt and pour soap base that is made of Coconut Oil, Palm Oil, Safflower Oil, Glycerin (kosher, of vegetable origin), Purified Water, Sodium Hydroxide (saponifying agent), Sorbitol (moisturizer), Sorbitan oleate (emulsifier), and Soy bean protein (conditioner). I purchase this online and it typically runs about $30 for ten pounds. That may sound expensive, however, if you consider, that most bars of soap only weigh about six ounces, if you make the soap yourself, it is going to cost you a mere $0.19 per ounce. This means that you can purchase the soap base and it will cost you about $1.20 for a typical sized bar of soap. When you add in the oils that you have made yourself, you might have an additional couple of dollars in the bar of soap, but the fact that you made the soap, with your own hands, and your own energy, makes up for any additional cost you may incur. The items you will need are as follows:

- ☆ Melt and Pour Soap Base
- ☆ Any essential oils you need for the magickal purpose of the soap
- ☆ And herbs you wish to add to the soap
- ☆ Soap colorants – if you wish to add color energy to the soap
- ☆ Glass measuring cups, at least 2 cup size, and you will need one for oils and one for herbs

- ★ Large non-serrated knife with a thin blade (I like to use filet knives because they are sharp and thin)
- ★ Eyedroppers
- ★ Cutting board
- ★ Several spoons
- ★ Spray bottle
- ★ Plastic wrap
- ★ Paper towels
- ★ Cooking spray – preferably not flavored
- ★ Plastic or rubber bendable molds if you want shapes or a small, glass, square baking dish

When you purchase the soap base, it will come with instructions on melting, however, I just use the microwave. You will need to melt out one and a half cups of melted soap base in each measuring cup. Lightly spray whatever you are using as a mold for the soap with the cooking spray and wipe any excess out with the paper towels. Combine any herbs that you have gathered in a bowl and add them to one of the cups of soap base and stir well, while you visualize your intent and final goal. Combine the oils that you have gathered and add them to the other cup of melted soap base and stir well, while you visualize your intent and final goal. If you are using colorants you will add equal amounts to both cups, and again you will need to stir well and visualize your intent and final goal. Once you have each cup of soap base mixed well, you can mix them together by pouring them simultaneously into the mold that you have chose. As you pour the soap into the mold, visualize your intent pouring into the mold with the soap. Give the soap base a final stir, again visualizing your intent and final goals and set it aside for it to cool and harden. Once the soap has hardened (time depends on the size and shape of the mold, and environmental temperature) you can remove it from the mold. If you have chosen a square cake dish, you will use your knife to cut the mold into squares that are easier to handle. Once you have the larger mold cut down into smaller, more manageable pieces, you can then use the plastic wrap to tightly wrap the individual bars of soap so that you can store them away for later use.

When you are ready to use your soap, you may wish to hold the soap in your hands as you again visualize the intent you have for the ritual bath so you can empower the soap some more. Then you are ready to use your homemade ritual soap.

Tinctures

As we all know, using oils in ritual aids magick by the smell they emit as well as by lending their energies. Tinctures do the same thing and are just as effective. Tinctures are created by soaking dried herbs in alcohol. The process of making tinctures can be just as time consuming as making essential oils but tinctures do not seem to go rancid like essential oils can. But as with making most things magickal, there is a catch! There always has to be a catch does there not? When you make tinctures, you cannot use just any ol' alcohol. You have to use ethyl alcohol, which is also known as ethanol or grain alcohol. Rubbing alcohol is made from petroleum products, and the extremely sharp odor makes it impossible to use to capture the scents of your herbs. So do not try rubbing alcohol, it is a waste of time, energy, money and herbs.

Ethyl alcohol can be difficult to find and it can be expensive. You will need alcohol that is at least seventy percent pure or 140 proof. Most of the vodka's that you will find in liquor stores are only 90 proof which is forty-five percent pure, so these will not work. This will take some time, leg work and research to locate the ethyl alcohol, but once you find it you will be ready to begin making your tinctures.

Finding the ethyl alcohol is the hardest part of making tinctures. You will need to begin with a good amount of dried herbs. Fresh herbs will not work with tinctures because of their natural water content. There are also some plants that will just not work at all with alcohol because they are not soluble in alcohol which means their natural scent will not transfer into the alcohol. There is a list of recommended tincturing herbs in the back of the book that you can refer to when preparing your tinctures. Use that list as a starting point, and research and experiment on your own to see if you find any different results. That list is one that I have comprised over my years of making tinctures and these are the ones that have worked for me.

Once you have your herbs gathered, you will need to grind them into the finest powder possible. If you are going to be using woods, it may be a good idea to see if you can purchase them in powder form. You will then need to empower your herbs. Visualize your goal and pour the herbs into a small bottle with a tight fitting lid. Then, pour in just enough alcohol to completely wet and cover the herbs in the bottle and place the cap on tightly. Shake the bottle vigorously everyday for the next week. As you shake the bottle, be sure to visualize your goals and intent as this will further empower the tincture as it brews. After the herbs have brewed in the alcohol for a week, use a coffee filter set in a strainer to strain the alcohol. If the scent is strong enough at this point, then the tincture is finished and you can pour the alcohol back into the bottle and close the cap tightly. If the scent is not strong enough at this point, add the herbs again, and repeat the process above – shaking vigorously everyday for the next week. Continue this process until the scent is where you want it. To truly test the tincture, you will need to put a drop or two on your wrist, and wait for the alcohol to evaporate then smell the aroma. If after two or three rounds of straining and adding more herbs you have found that there is little or no smell, you are using an herb that is not soluble in alcohol. Once the tincture is as you want it, add three to five drops of castor oil or glycerin to the tincture to stabilize and hold the smell. Place a label on the bottle and store it in a cool, dark and dry place

To use your tinctures, you need to remember one thing: ***NEVER EVER DRINK A TINCTURE!!!*** You can use the tinctures you have made to make your scented incense papers, you can anoint your body or magickal tools, or virtually any other use that you would have for magickal oils.

Tools of a Witch

As with most other religions, tools are used in witchcraft to aid and enhance ritual worship. Tools have no power in and of themselves, though they do have powerful symbolic significances. Some, like the Wand and Athame (pronounced ath-*ay*-me), are used to invoke and direct whatever power you generate or pass through them.

While tools are not absolutely necessary to the practice of the craft, some tools are nice to have if only to focus our will and concentration. The basic tools to start with are the elemental tools or those tools which represent the four elements of life: The Pentacle for Earth, The Wand for Air, The Athame for Fire and The Chalice for Water.

Tools need not be purposely bought or excessively expensive. Take a look around your house, many ordinary implements can be used or improvised as tools. You could even make your own and by doing so, a certain amount of personal power will be infused into the item, thus increasing its effectiveness.

All tools as they are collected should be cleansed of all negative energies and past use influences. This is very important because you have no idea what the tool was used for or by who in its past and you do not want that to bleed over into your workings. To cleanse a magickal tool, you will need to physically clean the item, while visualizing the tools current energies evaporating from the tool. Once you are satisfied that the tool is clean, you will then need to bury the tool in the Earth for at least three days to allow the earth to purify the tool. Not all tools that you acquire will be small enough to bury in the ground. Especially if you are like me and a lot of your magickal tools are actually small kitchen appliances. If you are unable to bury a tool, do not fret. Simply gather some dirt from outside and either place it in a consecrated bowl on top of the item or in the item.

If using dirt is not a method that you feel comfortable with, you can use water instead, again depending on the type of item you are cleansing. It is preferred that natural water, such as ocean, lake or river water be used. If you cannot use one of these types of water, simply obtain some sea salt to place in the water, and then submerge the item for at least three hours. Be sure to use common sense since you do not want to ruin the item. Do whatever seems appropriate for each item. After the cleansing process, each tool needs to be consecrated before it is ready to use for magickal purposes.

Below is a list of the standard tools used in witchcraft along with their uses.

Athame - The athame is the traditional ritual dagger of the witch. Commonly it has a black handle and steel double-edged blade. Many Witches will engrave the handle or blade with magickal symbols indicative of deities, spirits or the elements as sources of power. The athame is a tool of command; it is used to direct the power you pass through it. It is used to cast circles by tracing the circumference, to charge and consecrate objects and banish negative energies. In most traditions, it is never used as a mundane knife for cutting purposes, and is used strictly for magickal purposes only. As elemental tools of the craft, in most traditions it is associated with the element of Fire; however there are other traditions where the athame represents Air. The phallic symbolism of the knife links it with the God.

Pentacle - The pentacle is a traditional tool of the craft. Originally it is thought to have been adopted from ceremonial magic. It is usually a round solid disc often made from stone, wood or cooper. On the disc is engraved or painted an up-right five pointed star enclosed inside a circle. In some traditions other symbols are added indicative of deities, spirits or the elements as sources of power. The pentacle is normally the centerpiece of the alter on which objects are placed to be consecrated or charged, such things as amulets, charms and tools are placed on it, as is the salt and water for blessing. The pentacle represents the element of Earth and is sometimes used to summon the Gods and Goddesses.

Wand - The wand is one of the prime magical tools of the witch. Traditionally the wand is made from the wood of a sacred tree. These include the Willow, Elder, Oak, Apple, Peach, Hazel and Cherry, to mention just a few. Its length should approximate the crook of the elbow to the middle of the index finger. These days many modern materials are used instead, and even tipped with crystals and gems. The wand is a tool of invocation; it is used to evoke the Gods, Goddesses and Spirits. It is also used to bestow blessings, charge objects and draw down the moon during ritual. In most traditions the wand represents the element of Air, however there other traditions where the wand will represent Fire.

Censer - The censer is an incense burner used to contain burning incense during ritual. Any type of censer can be used, even a simple bowl filled with sand will do. The censer represents the element of Air and is normally placed before the images of the Goddess and God on the altar.

Chalice - The Chalice is one of the four elemental tools of witchcraft and represents the element of Water. It is a symbol of containment and often represents the womb of the Goddess. The base is symbolic of the material world, the stem symbolizes the connection between man and spirit and the rim or opening symbolically receives spiritual energy.

The chalice can be made of any material, in times of old - Horns, Shells and Gourds were used to hold sacred liquids during ritual, and then in later times - Silver became the preferred material, having long been associated with the moon and the Goddess. The chalice is used to hold the blessed water and wine during ritual. It is traditional in many covens to pass the chalice around to all members, who then take a drink as a token of unity.

Broom - The broom is a ritual tool of the witch, sacred to both Goddess and the God. It is sacred to the God - through its symbolic phallic shape and is sacred to the Goddess - through its three-piece make up, the stick, brush and binding cord being symbolic of the triformis aspect of the Goddess. Traditionally the broom was made from three different woods: Ash for the handle, Birch twigs for the brush and Willow for the binding cord. Ash is protective and has command over the four elements. Birch is purifying and draws spirits to one's service. Willow is sacred to the Goddess. The broom is used for a variety of purposes but most generally to purify and protect. It is used to ritually cleanse an area before magick is performed by symbolically sweeping away negative energies and astral build up. Of old it was used to guard the home and persons within against psychic attack or evil curses by placing it across the threshold, windowsills or doorways. It was also placed under the bed or a pillow to protect the sleeper. Traditionally and perhaps the use which most people identify it with, are the old wedding ceremonies of the Gypsies and the early American slaves, where a couple leapt over the broom to ensure fertility, domestic harmony and longevity. Today pagan hand-fasting rituals often include a broom jump.

Boline - The Boline or White-Handled knife as it is now known is the practical knife of the craft. Traditionally it was used to harvest herbs and had a blade in the form of a small sickle. Today it is normally a mundane knife used for cutting and carving. It has a white handle to differentiate it from the Athame, which has a black handle and is used only for magickal purposes. The boline is used to cut wands and herbs, to mark and carve candles with symbols and to cut cords for use in magick. Any other ritual function requiring the use of a knife, such as cutting flowers for the altar, can be performed with the boline.

Cauldron - The cauldron is probably the tool most associated with witchcraft and is steeped in magickal tradition and mystery. The cauldron is the container in which transmutation, germination, and transformations may occur. It is symbolic of the womb of the Goddess, and is the manifested essence of femininity and fertility. Everything is born from the cauldron of the Goddess and afterwards everything returns back to it. It is also symbolic of the element of water, as well as reincarnation, immortality and inspiration. In ritual the cauldron is used as a container for making brews and potions, or to contain a small fire for use with spells. It can also be used for scrying (divination) by filling it with water and gazing into its depths. In ancient times the cauldron was used as a cooking vessel and for brew making. Traditionally it was made from cast iron; it rests on three legs and has an opening smaller then its widest part. Cauldrons are made in many sizes but can be difficult to find, so you will need to persevere if you want one. Remember, they can be expensive not only to buy but to ship as well because they can be quite heavy the larger they are.

Bell - The bell is a ritual tool of invocation and banishment. The bell is a feminine symbol of the creative force, that of the Goddess. The bell can be rung to indicate the start of a rite by banishing negative influences before the ritual begins. Often it is used to invoke the Goddess during ritual, or sounded at the four quarters to call forth such spirits as the Watchers and Elementals. Bells can be used to guard the home by warding off evil spells and spirits, or evoking good energies when placed in cupboards or hung on doors. Hung from a cord the bell symbolizes the human soul suspended between heaven and earth.

Book of Shadows - The Book of Shadows is the workbook of the witch. In it is recorded: Rituals guidelines, Invocations, Spells, Runes, Rules of a particular Coven or Tradition, Symbols, Poems, Chants, and anything else of use to the witch during ritual. Traditionally the Book of Shadows was always hand written by the individual. A common custom for new initiates into a Coven, is to hand copy his teacher's Book of Shadows exactly as it appeared, then later to add his own material as he progressed in the craft. Today with the advantages of technology they are often typed and photocopied, or even computerized onto flash drives. To make your own Book of Shadows, you can use any form of blank book, but perhaps the best type to use are those of a loose-leaf nature, thus allowing pages to be shuffled around when preparing for rituals. My personal Book of Shadows is made of wood, and constructed in the same manner as many scrapbooks that you would purchase from a hobby store so that I can add as many pages as necessary.

Sabbats

There is so much information about the Sabbats that a book could be written about these eight days and it could end up being quite lengthy (hmmmm, maybe a project I can tackle for the next seven years). So what I am going to include here will just be the name of the Sabbat, a brief description of the events that generally take place in my home and the date of the Sabbat.

Yule: Midwinter, commonly known as Yule, is generally celebrated on or around December 21st. In my house, we start celebrating six days before, and we give a gift to each member of the house, including our pets for each of those six days. I generally prepare a large meal on Yule that consists of ham, lots of veggies and wine. The house is decorated with evergreens such as holly, pine and mistletoe.

    Imbolc: Imbolc takes place on or around February 2nd. Imbolc is a time of purification and cleansing. This is also when we begin our spring cleaning in our house. Spring cleaning lasts until Ostara for us. This is also when we make our pledges and rededications for the coming year.

    Ostara: Ostara takes place on or around March 20th. This is when we celebrate fertility, not only within ourselves but for the animals and the crops to come. We decorate eggs and hide them for the little ones to find.

    Beltane: Beltane takes place on or around May 1st and this is when we celebrate death and rebirth. We celebrate the union of the Mother Goddess and her young Horned god. We build a bonfire, that usually is quite large and it is started with nine sacred woods: oak, apple, hawthorn, birth, ash, willow, cedar, yew and holly. After the fire has gone out and the ashes have cooled we will spread those ashes over our crops. This is also a time that we commune with the fairies, something that is very popular amongst the children. We also dance around the May Pole.

Midsummer/Litha: Midsummer takes place on June 21st. We spend this day hiking and swimming. As the day starts to fade we will enjoy a spicy dinner, where the main course is pork as this is sacred to Cerridwen.

Lammas/Lughsnasadh: Lammas takes place on August 1st. We decorate the altar and house with grains and a favorite food for us at this time is the blooming onion. The onion is sacred to the sun. We will have a picnic where we can leave libations to the earth of whole grain breads and fruit wines.

Mabon: This is the Witches Thanksgiving and it takes place on September 21st. We will make grapevine wreaths that are wrapped with gold and yellow ribbons. We also make Witch's brooms out of corn husks.

Samhain: Samhain takes place on October 31st and this is our New Years Eve. This is also when we honor those who have passed. We make our new resolutions for the year to come, carve jack-o-lanterns and light them up with a spirit candle and we have a mute supper.

Correspondences

In the following pages you will find various correspondences that are meant to aid you in performing your spell work. The information contained within these lists is not meant to be all inclusive, rather a starting point for your research and practice. You may find that some of the items listed here do not work for you as they have for me, and you may find that other items work in ways that I have not listed. We are all different, and we all emit different energies, so it is very possible that certain herbs may react differently to you.

Each set of correspondences will have two parts. The first part will contain the item followed by its magickal property. The second part will contain the magickal property followed by all of the items that match that property.

Following this section will be a section that is dedicated to magickal writings, such as the Charge of the God and Goddess, the Wiccan Rede, and the 13 Principles of Wiccan Belief.

Colors

Black – returning to sender, negative work, protection, divination

Blue – protection

Brown – peace in the home, herbal magick, invoking Earth

Dark green – agriculture, financial, invoking the goddess of regeneration

Dark purple – government, calling forth the powers of the Ancient Ones

Gold – prosperity, sun magick, the Lord, attraction

Green – healing, cardinal point of North

Indigo – reveal deep secrets, defenses, protection on the astral plane

Lavender – invoking the righteous spirit within oneself while doing works of good

Light blue – protection of your home

Orange – material gain, attraction, sealing a spell

Pink – friendship, harmony, binding magick

Red – love, romance, energy, cardinal point of the South

Silver – the Lady, quick money, moon magick, invocation of the moon

White – righteousness, purity, devotional magick, can be used as a substitution for any other color

Yellow – healing, cardinal point of the East

Colors by Magickal Property

Agriculture: dark green

Attraction: gold, orange

Binding magick: pink

Calling forth the powers of the Ancient Ones: dark purple

Can be used as a substitution for any other color: white

Cardinal point of the East: yellow

Cardinal Point of North: green

Cardinal point of the South: red

Cardinal point of the West: blue

Defenses: indigo

Devotional magick: white

Divination: black

Energy: red

Financial: dark green

Friendship: pink

Government: dark purple

Harmony: pink

Healing: green, yellow

Invocation of the moon: silver

Invoking Earth: brown

Invoking the goddess of regeneration: dark green

Invoking the righteous spirit within oneself while doing works of good: lavender

Love: red

Material gain: orange

Moon magick: silver

Negative work: black

Peace in the home: brown

Prosperity: gold

Protection: black, blue

Protection of your home: light blue

Protection on the astral plane: indigo

Purity: white

Quick money: silver

Returning to sender: black

Reveal deep secrets: indigo

Righteousness: white

Romance: red

Sealing a spell: orange

Sun magick: gold

The Lady: silver

The Lord: gold

Flowers

With any type of plant, it is very important to remember that some of them can be very toxic not only to humans but to your pets as well. So before you plant any of the following plants, be sure that you check out the possible toxicity of the plant to either yourself or your pets if you have them. I have done a lot of research on these toxic plants and for the plants that I have listed here, I will use a (C) for cats, (D) for dogs and (H) for horses. I would strongly advise doing some research on your own to be sure that none of the other plants that I have not listed here are not toxic to you or your pets.

Crocus: newly blooming love, enhance visions, bring about intuitive dreams.

Daffodil (C) (D) (H): love, fertility, abundance, luck.

Dandelion: Leaf - healing, purification, ritual cleansing, positive change; Yellow flowers - divination, draw good energy

Echinacea (also called the purple coneflower): add a boost to charms and sachets, prosperity, offering to deities

Geranium (C) (D) (H): Love, healing

Goldenseal: money spells, business dealings, financial gain, and legal issues

Hibiscus (C) (D) (H): passion, attract love, lust, prophetic dreams about your lover

Holly (C) (D) (H): protection of the home

Hyacinth (C) (D) (H): patron herb of homosexual men, promotes peaceful sleep, guard against nightmares, heal a broken heart, ease grief when a loved one dies

Irish moss: Good fortune in business, gambling, good luck charm.

Ivy: Home and personal protection

Jasmine: Increases potency of love spells

Juniper: Attract new love, protection from thieves.

Lavender: Physical and emotional healing, peace in the home and marriage, purification

Lily (C) (D) (H): fertility, rebirth, renewal, abundance

Narcissus (C) (D) (H): promote polarity, harmony, tranquility, inner peace

Rose: love, romance, sex, fertility, healing emotions related to heartbreak

Sunflower: Fertility, joy, happiness, prosperity

Tulip (C) (D) (H): prosperity

Violet: tranquility, peace. The leaf offers protection from evil; the petals bring about luck and enhance nighttime magic.

Zinnia: To bring joy to your life and childlike innocence

Flowers by Magickal Property

With any type of plant, it is very important to remember that some of them can be very toxic not only to humans but to your pets as well. So before you plant any of the following plants, be sure that you check out the possible toxicity of the plant to either yourself or your pets if you have them. I have done a lot of research on these toxic plants and for the plants that I have listed here, I will use a (C) for cats, (D) for dogs and (H) for horses. I would strongly advise doing some research on your own to be sure that none of the other plants that I have not listed here are not toxic to you or your pets.

Abundance: daffodil (C) (D) (H), lily (C) (D) (H)

Add a boost to charms and sachets: Echinacea

Attract love: hibiscus (C) (D) (H)

Attract new love: juniper

Bring about intuitive dreams: crocus

Business dealings: goldenseal

Childlike innocence: zinnia

Divination: dandelion

Draw good energy: dandelion

Ease grief when a loved one dies: hyacinth (C) (D) (H)

Enhance nighttime magic: violet

Enhance visions: crocus

Fertility: daffodil (C) (D) (H), lily (C) (D) (H), rose, sunflower

Financial gain: goldenseal

Gambling: Irish moss

Good fortune in business: Irish moss

Good luck charm: Irish moss

Guard against nightmares: hyacinth (C) (D) (H)

Happiness: sunflower

Harmony: narcissus (C) (D) (H)

Heal a broken heart: hyacinth (C) (D) (H)

Healing: dandelion, geranium(C) (D) (H)

Healing emotions related to heartbreak: rose

Home protection: holly (C) (D) (H), ivy

Increases potency of love spells: jasmine

Inner peace: narcissus (C) (D) (H), violet

Joy: sunflower

Legal issues: goldenseal

Love: daffodil(C) (D) (H), geranium (C) (D) (H), rose

Luck: daffodil (C) (D) (H), violet

Lust: hibiscus (C) (D) (H)

Money spells: goldenseal

Newly blooming love: crocus

Offering to deities: Echinacea

Passion: hibiscus (C) (D) (H)

Patron herb of homosexual men: hyacinth (C) (D) (H)

Peace in the home and marriage: lavender

Peace: violet

Personal protection: ivy

Physical and emotional healing: lavender

Positive change: dandelion

Promote polarity: narcissus (C) (D) (H)

Promotes peaceful sleep: hyacinth (C) (D) (H)

Prophetic dreams about your lover: hibiscus (C) (D) (H)

Prosperity: Echinacea, sunflower, tulip(C) (D) (H)

Protection from evil: violet

Protection from thieves: juniper

Protection of the home: holly (C) (D) (H)

Purification: dandelion, lavender

Rebirth: lily (C) (D) (H)

Renewal: lily (C) (D) (H)

Ritual cleansing: dandelion

Romance: rose

Sex: rose

To bring joy to your life: zinnia

Tranquility: narcissus (C) (D) (H), violet

Gems and Stones
Not all of the gems and stones listed here will be easy to obtain. There are many that you can get from a

wonderful and very reputable company called Azure Green. I have been a customer of Azure Green since I became a Witch in 1992. If there is ANYTHING that I cannot find in a local store, www.azuregreen.com is the first website I go to.

Agate: Element - Various; Planet – Mercury; Magickal Properties – courage, gardening, healing, longevity, love, protection, strength

Alum: Element – Earth; Planet – Saturn; Magickal Properties – protection

Amazonite: Element – Earth; Planet – Uranus; Magickal Properties – gambling, success

Amber: Element – Fire; Planet – Sun; Magickal Properties – beauty, healing, love, luck, protection, strength

Amethyst: Element – Water; Planet – Jupiter, Neptune; Magickal Properties – courage, dreams, happiness, healing, love, overcoming alcoholism, peace, protection against thieves, psychism

Apache Tear: Element – Fire; Planet – Saturn; Magickal Properties – luck, protection

Aquamarine: Element – Water; Planet – Moon; Magickal Properties – courage, peace, psychism, purification

Aventurine: Element – Air; Planet – Mercury; Magickal Properties – eyesight, gambling, healing, luck, mental powers, money, peace

Azurite: Element – Water; Planet – Venus; Magickal Properties – divination, dreams, healing, psychism

Banded Agate: Element – Fire; Planet – Mercury; Magickal Properties – de-stress, protection, restore bodily energy

Beryl: Element – Water; Planet – Moon; Magickal Properties – anti-gossip, energy, healing, love, psychism

Black Agate: Element – Fire; Planet – Mercury; Magickal Properties – courage, protection, success

Black and White Agate: Element – Earth; Planet – Mercury; Magickal Properties – guard against physical danger

Black Tourmaline: Element – Earth; Planet – Saturn; Magickal Properties – grounding, protection

Blue Tourmaline: Element – Water; Planet – Venus; Magickal Properties – de-stress, peace, sleep

Bloodstone: Element – Fire; Planet – Mars; Magickal Properties – agriculture, business, courage, healing, invisibility, legal matters, power, strength, victory, wealth

Blue Calcite: Element – Water; Planet – Venus; Magickal Properties – healing, purification

Blue Lace Agate: Element – Water; Planet – Mercury; Magickal Properties – de-stress, happiness, peace

Brown Agate: Element – Fire; Planet – Mercury; Magickal Properties – guard against evil, success, victory, wealth

Brown Jasper: Element – Earth; Planet – Saturn; Magickal Properties – centering, grounding, psychism, spirituality

Calcite: Element – Various; Planet – Various; Magickal Properties – centering, energy, healing, love, money, peace, protection, purification, spirituality

Carnelian: Element – Fire; Planet – Sun; Magickal Properties – courage, eloquence, healing, protection, sexual energy

Cat's Eye: Element – Earth; Planet – Venus; Magickal Properties – beauty, gambling, healing, protection, wealth

Celestite: Element – Water; Planet – Venus, Neptune; Magickal Properties – compassion, eloquence, healing

Chalcedony: Element – Water; Planet – Moon; Magickal Properties – anti-nightmare, lactation, luck, peace, protection, travel

Chrysocolla: Element – Water; Planet – Venus; Magickal Properties – love, peace, wisdom

Chrysoprase: Element – Earth; Planet – Venus; Magickal Properties – friendship, happiness, healing, luck, money, success

Clear Calcite: Element – Water; Planet – Moon; Magickal properties – mediation, spirituality

Citrine: Element – Fire; Planet – Sun; Magickal Properties – anti-nightmare, protection, psychism

Coal: Element – Earth; Planet – Saturn; Magickal Properties – money

Coral: Element – Water; Planet – Venus; Magickal Properties – agriculture, healing, peace, protection, regulate menstruation, wisdom

Crystal Quartz: Element – Fire, Water; Planet – Sun, Moon; Magickal Properties – healing, lactation, power, protection, psychism

Diamond: Element – Fire; Planet – Sun; Magickal Properties – courage, healing, peace, protection, reconciliation, sexual dysfunction, spirituality, strength

Emerald: Element – Earth; Planet – Venus; Magickal Properties – eyesight, exorcism, love, mental powers, money, protection, psychism

Flint: Element – Fire; Planet – Mars; Magickal Properties – divination, healing, protection

Garnet: Element – Fire; Planet – Mars; Magickal Properties – healing, protection, strength

Green Agate: Element – Earth; Planet – Mercury; Magickal Properties – healthy eyes

Green Calcite: Element – Earth; Planet – Venus; Magickal Properties – money, prosperity

Green Jasper: Element – Earth; Planet – Venus; Magickal Properties – healing, sleep

Green Tourmaline: Element – Earth; Planet – Venus; Magickal Properties – creativity, money, success

Hematite: Element – Fire; Planet – Saturn; Magickal Properties – divination, grounding, healing

Jade: Element – Water; Planet – Venus; Magickal Properties – gardening, healing, longevity, love, money, prosperity, protection, wisdom

Jasper: Element – Various; Planet – Various; Magickal Properties – beauty, healing, protection

Jet: Element – Earth; Planet – Saturn; Magickal Properties – anti-nightmare, divination, health, luck, protection

Kunzite: Element – Earth; Planet – Venus; Magickal Properties – grounding, peace, relaxation

Lapis Lazuli: Element – Water; Planet – Venus; Magickal Properties – courage, fidelity, healing, joy, love, protection, psychism

Lava: Element – Fire; Planet – Mars; Magickal Properties – protection

Lepidolite: Element – Water; Planet – Jupiter, Neptune; Magickal Properties – anti-nightmare, love, luck, protection, psychism, spirituality

Malachite: Element – Earth; Planet – Venus; Magickal Properties – business success, love, peace, power, protection

Marble: Element – Water; Planet – Moon; Magickal Properties – protection, success

Mica: Element – Air; Planet – Mercury; Magickal Properties – divination, protection

Moonstone: Element – Water; Planet – Moon; Magickal Properties – dieting, divination, gardening, love, protection, psychism, sleep, youth

Mother-of-Pearl: Element – Water; Planet – Moon, Neptune; Magickal Properties – protection, wealth

Moss Agate: Element – Earth; Planet – Mercury; Magickal Properties – happiness, healing

Mottled Jasper: Element – Air; Planet – Mercury; Magickal Properties – control, protection

Obsidian: Element – Fire; Planet – Saturn; Magickal Properties – divination, grounding, peace, protection

Olivine: Element – Earth; Planet – Venus; Magickal Properties – love, luck, money, protection

Onyx: Element – Fire; Planet – Mars, Saturn; Magickal Properties – defensive magick, protection, reducing sexual desires

Opal: Element – All elements; Planet – All planets; Magickal Properties – astral projection, beauty, luck, power, psychism

Orange Calcite: Element – Fire; Planet – Sun; Magickal Properties – energy, protection

Pearl: Element – Water; Planet – Moon; Magickal Properties – love, luck, money, protection

Peridot: Element – Earth; Planet – Venus; Magickal Properties – health, protection, sleep, wealth

Pink Calcite: Element – Water; Planet – Venus; Magickal Properties – calming, centering, grounding, love

Pink Tourmaline: Element – Water; Planet – Venus; Magickal Properties – friendship, love, sympathy

Pipestone: Element – Fire; Planet – Mars, Sun; Magickal Properties – healing, peace

Pumice: Element – Air; Planet – Mercury; Magickal Properties – banishment, ease childbirth, protection

Red Agate: Element – Fire; Planet – Mercury; Magickal Properties – calming, healing, promote peace

Red Jasper: Element – Fire; Planet – Mars; Magickal Properties – beauty, defensive magick, grace, healing, protection, return negativity

Red Tourmaline: Element – Fire; Planet – Mars; Magickal Properties – courage, energy, protection, strengthen will

Rhodocrosite: Element – Fire; Planet – Mars; Magickal Properties –energy, love, peace

Rhodonite: Element – Fire; Planet – Mars; Magickal Properties – anti-confusion, peace

Ruby: Element – Fire; Planet – Mars; Magickal Properties – anti-nightmare, joy, power, protection, wealth

Sapphire: Element – Water; Planet – Moon; Magickal Properties – defensive magick, healing, love, meditation, money, peace, power, psychism

Sard: Element – Fire; Planet – Mars; Magickal Properties – courage, easing childbirth, love, protection

Sardonyx: Element – Fire; Planet – Mars; Magickal Properties – courage, eloquence, luck, marital happiness, peace, protection

Selenite: Element – Water; Planet – Moon; Magickal Properties – energy, reconciliation

Serpentine: Element – Fire; Planet – Saturn; Magickal Properties – lactation, protection

Sodalite: Element – Water; Planet – Venus; Magickal Properties – healing, peace, meditation, wisdom

Sphene: Element – Air; Planet – Mercury; Magickal Properties – mental powers, spirituality

Sugilite: Element – Water; Planet – Jupiter; Magickal Properties – healing, psychism, spirituality, wisdom

Sulfur: Element – Fire; Planet – Sun; Magickal Properties – healing, protection

Sunstone: Element – Fire; Planet – Sun; Magickal Properties – energy, health, protection, sexual energy

Tiger's Eye: Element – Fire; Planet – Sun; Magickal Properties – courage, divination, energy, luck, protection

Topaz: Element – Fire; Planet – Sun; Magickal Properties – healing, money, love, protection, weight loss

Tourmaline: Element – Various; Planet – Various; Magickal Properties – astral projection, business, courage, energy, friendship, health, love, money, peace

Turquoise: Element – Earth; Planet – Venus, Neptune; Magickal Properties – courage, friendship, healing, love, luck, money, protection

Watermelon Tourmaline: Element – Fire, Water; Planet – Mars, Venus; Magickal Properties – attract love, energy

Zircon: Element – Fire; Planet – Sun; Magickal Properties – anti-theft, beauty, healing, love, peace, protection, sexual energy

Gems and Stones by Magickal Property

Not all of the gems and stones listed here will be easy to obtain. There are many that you can get from a wonderful and very reputable company called Azure

Green. I have been a customer of Azure Green since I became a Witch in 1992. If there is ANYTHING that I cannot find in a local store, www.azuregreen.com is the first website I go to.

Agriculture: bloodstone, coral

Anti-confusion: rhodonite

Anti-gossip: beryl

Anti-nightmare: chalcedony, citrine, jet, lepidolite, ruby

Anti-theft: zircon

Astral projection: opal, tourmaline

Attract love: watermelon tourmaline

Banishment: pumice

Beauty: amber, cat's eye, jasper, opal, red jasper, zircon

Business: bloodstone, tourmaline

Business success: malachite

Calming: pink calcite, red agate

Centering: brown jasper, calcite, pink calcite

Compassion: celestite

Control: mottled jasper

Courage: agate, amethyst, aquamarine, black agate, bloodstone, carnelian, diamond, lapis lazuli, red tourmaline, sard, sardonyx, tiger's eye, turquoise

Creativity: green tourmaline

Defensive magick: onyx, red jasper, sapphire

De-stress: banded agate, blue tourmaline, blue lace agate

Dieting: moonstone

Divination: azurite, flint, hematite, jet, mica, moonstone, obsidian, tiger's eye

Dreams: amethyst, azurite

Ease childbirth: pumice, sard

Elements: <u>AIR</u> – aventurine, mica, mottled jasper, opal, pumice, sphene; <u>FIRE</u> – amber, apache tear, banded agate, black agate, bloodstone, brown agate, carnelian, citrine, crystal quartz, diamond, flint, garnet, hematite, lava, obsidian, onyx, opal, orange calcite, pipestone, red agate, red jasper, red tourmaline, rhodocrosite, rhodonite, ruby, sard, sardonyx, serpentine, sulfur, sunstone, tiger's eye, topaz, watermelon tourmaline, zircon; <u>WATER</u> – amethyst, aquamarine, azurite, beryl, blue tourmaline, blue calcite, blue lace agate, celestite, chalcedony, chrysocolla, clear calcite, coral, jade, lapis lazuli, ledpidolite, marble, moonstone, mother of pearl, opal, pearl, pink calcite, pink tourmaline, sapphire, selenite, sodalite, sugilite; <u>EARTH</u> – alum, amazonite, black and white agate, black tourmaline, brown jasper, cat's eye, chrysoprase, emerald, green agate, green calcite, green jasper, green tourmaline, jet, kunzite, malachite, moss agate, olivine, opal, peridot, turquoise

Eloquence: carnelian, Celestite, sardonyx

Energy: beryl, calcite, orange calcite, red tourmaline, rhodocrosite, selenite, sunstone, tiger's eye, tourmaline, watermelon tourmaline

Exorcism: emerald

Eyesight: aventurine, emerald

Fidelity: lapis lazuli

Friendship: chrysoprase, pink tourmaline, tourmaline, turquoise

Gambling: amazonite, aventurine, cat's eye

Gardening: agate, jade, moonstone

Grace: red jasper

Grounding: black tourmaline, brown jasper, hematite, kunzite, obsidian, pink calcite

Guard against evil: brown agate

Guard against physical danger: black and white agate

Happiness: amethyst, blue lace agate, chrysoprase, moss agate

Healing: agate, amber, amethyst, aventurine, azurite, beryl, bloodstone, blue calcite, calcite, carnelian, cat's eye, Celestite, chrysoprase, coral, crystal quartz, diamond, flint, garnet, green jasper, hematite, jade, jasper, lapis lazuli, moss agate, pipestone, red agate, red jasper, sapphire, sodalite, sugilite, sulfur, topaz, turquoise, zircon

Health: jet, peridot, sunstone, tourmaline

Healthy eyes: green agate

Invisibility: bloodstone

Joy: lapis lazuli, ruby

Lactation: chalcedony, crystal quartz, serpentine

Legal matters: bloodstone

Longevity: agate, jade

Love: agate, alexandrite, amber, amethyst, beryl, calcite, chrysocolla, emerald, jade, lapis lazuli, lepidolite, malachite, moonstone, olivine, pearl, pink calcite, pink tourmaline, rhodocrosite, sapphire, sard, topaz, tourmaline, turquoise, watermelon tourmaline, zircon

Luck: alexandrite, amber, apache tear, aventurine, chalcedony, chrysoprase, jet, lepidolite, olivine, opal, pearl, sardonyx, tiger's eye, turquoise

Marital happiness: sardonyx

Meditation: sapphire, sodalite

Mental powers: aventurine, emerald, sphene

Money: aventurine, calcite, chrysoprase, coral, emerald, green calcite, green tourmaline, jade, olivine, pearl, sapphire, topaz, tourmaline, turquoise

Overcoming alcoholism: amethyst

Peace: amethyst, aquamarine, aventurine, blue tourmaline, blue lace agate, calcite, chalcedony, chrysocolla, coral, diamond, kunzite, malachite, obsidian, pipestone, red agate, rhodocrosite, rhodonite, sapphire, sardonyx, sodalite, tourmaline, zircon

Planets: <u>JUPITER</u> – amethyst, lepidolite, sugalite; <u>MARS</u> – bloodstone, flint, garnet, lava, onyx, pipestone, red jasper, red tourmaline, rhodocrosite, rhodonite, ruby, sard, sardonyx, tourmaline; <u>MERCURY</u> – agate, aventurine, banded agate, black agate, black and white agate, blue lace agate, brown agate, green agate, mica, moss agate, mottled jasper, pumice, red agate, sphene; <u>MOON</u> - aquamarine, beryl, chalcedony, clear calcite, crystal quartz, marble, moonstone, mother of pearl, pearl, sapphire, selenite; <u>NEPTUNE</u> – amethyst, Celestite, lepidolite, mother of pearl, turquoise; <u>SATURN</u> – alum, apache tear, black tourmaline, brown jasper, coral, hematite, jet, obsidian, onyx, serpentine; <u>SUN</u> – amber, carnelian, citrine, crystal quartz, diamond, orange calcite, pipestone, sulfur, sunstone, tiger's eye, topaz, zircon; <u>URANUS</u> – amazonite; <u>VENUS</u> – azurite, blue tourmaline, blue calcite, cat's eye, Celestite, chrysocolla, chrysoprase, coral, emerald, green calcite, green jasper, green tourmaline, jade, kunzite, lapis lazuli, malachite, olivine, peridot, pink calcite, pink tourmaline, sodalite, turquoise, tourmaline

Power: bloodstone, crystal quartz, malachite, opal, ruby, sapphire

Promote peace: red agate

Prosperity: green calcite, jade

Protection: agate, alum, amber, apache tear, banded agate, black agate, black tourmaline, calcite, carnelian, cat's eye, chalcedony, citrine, coral, crystal quartz, diamond, emerald, flint, garnet, jade, jasper, jet, lapis lazuli, lava, lepidolite, malachite, marble, mica, moonstone, mother of pearl, moss agate, obsidian, olivine, onyx, orange calcite, pearl, peridot, pumice, red jasper, red tourmaline, ruby, sard, sardonyx, serpentine, sulfur, sunstone, tiger's eye, topaz, turquoise, zircon

Protection against thieves: amethyst

Psychism: amethyst, aquamarine, azurite, beryl, brown jasper, citrine, crystal quartz, emerald, lapis lazuli, lepidolite, moonstone, opal, sapphire, sugilite

Purification: aquamarine, blue calcite, calcite

Reconciliation: diamond, selenite

Reducing sexual desires: onyx

Regulate menstruation: coral

Relaxation: kunzite

Restore bodily energy: banded agate

Return negativity: red jasper

Sexual dysfunction: diamond

Sexual energy: carnelian, sunstone, zircon

Sleep: blue tourmaline, green jasper, moonstone, peridot

Spirituality: brown jasper, calcite, clear calcite, diamond, lepidolite, sphene, sugilite

Strength: agate, amber, bloodstone, diamond, garnet

Strengthen will: red tourmaline

Success: amazonite, black agate, brown agate, chrysoprase, green tourmaline, malachite, marble

Sympathy: pink tourmaline

Travel: chalcedony

Victory: bloodstone, brown agate

Wealth: bloodstone, brown agate, cat's eye, mother of pearl, peridot, ruby

Weight loss: topaz

Wisdom: chrysocolla, coral, jade, sodalite, sugilite

Youth: moonstone

Herbs

All of the following herbs can be purchased at your local grocery store. Remember that ROSEMARY can be used as a substitute for any herb. Also, the correspondences here are not completely inclusive. There will be many other uses for these herbs that you may discover on your own either through more research or through your own workings.

Allspice: Element – Fire, Earth; Planet – Mars, Venus; Magickal Properties – communication, compassion, determination, energy, healing, luck, money, prosperity

Almond: Element – Air; Planet – Mercury, Venus; Magickal properties – compassion, fertility, money, prosperity, wisdom

Alum: Element – Earth; Planet – Saturn; Magickal properties – protection from evil

Anise: Element – Air; Planet – Mercury, Jupiter; Magickal Properties – clairvoyance, cleansing, consecration, contacting other planes, divination, fertility, gain, good luck, happiness, love, money, passion, preventing nightmares, protection, psychic development, psychic protection, purification, weddings

Apple: Element – Water; Planet – Venus; Magickal properties – friendship, immortality, love

Avocado: Element – Water; Planet – Jupiter, Venus; Magickal properties – beauty, love, sex

Banana: Element – Water; Planet – Venus; Magickal properties – fertility, prosperity

Barley: Element – Earth; Planet – Venus; Magickal properties – love, protection

Basil: Element – Fire; Planet – Mars; Magickal properties – clairvoyance, commanding, consecration, courage, divination, exorcism, fertility, fidelity, good luck, grieving, happiness, harmony, hatred, honesty, Imbolc, initiation, inspiration, invocation, love, money, passion, peace, prevent theft, prosperity, protection, psychic development, psychic protection, purification, rituals for the dead, spell breaking, strength, success, tranquility, winter rituals

Bay leaves: Element – Fire; Planet – Sun; Magickal properties – clairvoyance, consecration, divination, dreams, endings, exorcism, good luck, harmony, healing, Imbolc, inspiration, justice, knowledge, love, magick, memory, money, overcome opposition, passion, peace, protection, psychic development, psychic protection, purification, release, spell breaking, strength, success, tranquility, transformation, winter rituals, wisdom, wishes, Yule

Blackberry: Element – Water; Planet – Venus; Magickal properties – healing, prosperity, protection

Blueberry: Element – Air; Planet – Jupiter; Magickal Properties - protection

Caraway seeds: Element – Air; Planet – Mercury; Magickal Properties – consecration, fertility, fidelity, gain, health, honesty, keeping secrets, love, memory, mental ability, passion, peace of mind, preventing theft, protection, retention, sensuality, sex, weddings

Cardamom: Element – Water; Planet – Venus, Mars; Magickal properties – enhance fertility, love, sexual energy

Carrot: Element – Earth, Fire; Planet - Mars; Magickal properties – fertility, sex

Catnip: Element – Water; Planet – Venus; Magickal properties – attract good spirits, beauty,

Cat magick, celebration, happiness, love, luck

Celery Seed: Element – Earth; Planet – Saturn, Mercury; Magickal properties – beauty, divination, fertility, love, mental ability, passion, psychic development, sex

Chili pepper: Element - Fire; Planet - Mars; Magickal properties – counteracting hexes, fidelity, love

Chive: Element – Fire; Planet – Mars; Magickal properties – protection against disease and evil influences

Cinnamon: Element – Air, Fire; Planet – Mercury, Sun, Mars, Uranus; Magickal properties – clairvoyance, communication, consecration, divination, energy, good luck, happiness, harmony, healing, inspiration, knowledge, love, meditation, money, passion, peace, prosperity, protection, psychic development, purification, sex, spirituality, success, tranquility, wisdom

Cloves: Element – Fire; Planet – Sun, Jupiter; Magickal properties – clairvoyance, cleansing, divination, exorcism, friendship, keeps away negative forces, love, memory, money, passion, peace of mind, prosperity, protection, psychic development, psychic protection, purification, release, spell breaking, stopping gossip

Coconut: Element – Water; Planet – Moon; Magickal Properties – chastity, protection, purification

Coriander (also called Cilantro): Element – Fire; Planet – Mars; Magickal properties – clairvoyance, divination, fertility, gain, health, keeping secrets, love, passion, peace, protection, retention, and weddings

Cucumber: Element - Water; Planet - Moon; Magickal properties – chastity, fertility, healing,

Cumin: Element – Fire; Planet – Mars; Magickal properties – exorcism, fidelity, longevity, love, peace, protection of ones home, protection

Curry: Element – Fire; Planet – Mars; Magickal properties – protection, repel evil at night

Dill Weed: Element – Earth, Fire; Planet – Mercury; Magickal properties – blessings, confidence, determination, dreams, fertility, gain, harmony, keeping secrets, love, money, passion, peace, prevents theft, prosperity, protection, psychic protection, rest, retention, sex, sleep, tranquility

Fennel: Element – Air, Fire; Planet – Mercury; Magickal properties – commanding, confidence, consecration, courage, divination, energy, fertility, gain, healing, longevity, love, meditation, Midsummer, money, protection, psychic protection, purification, strength, Summer rituals, virility

Flax: Element – Fire; Planet – Mercury; Magickal properties – healing, prosperity, protection, psychic powers

Garlic: Element – Fire; Planet – Mars; Magickal properties – clairvoyance, commanding, confidence, consecration, courage, divination, exorcism, fair weather, healing, longevity, magick, money, overcoming opposition, passion, prevents nightmares, protection, purification, sex, spell breaking, stopping gossip, strength, success

Ginger: Element – Fire; Planet – Mars; Magickal properties – binding, cursing, health, love, passion, power, prosperity, psychic development, psychic protection, sensuality, success

Grape: Element – Water; Planet – Moon; Magickal properties – fertility, mental ability, prosperity

Leek: Element – Fire; Planet – Mars; Magickal properties – protection,

Lemon: Element – Water; Planet – Moon; Magickal properties – friendship, longevity, love, moon magick, purification

Lemon grass: Element – Air; Planet – Mercury; Magickal properties – lust, psychic powers, repel snakes, sex

Lettuce: Element – Water; Planet – Moon; Magickal properties – protection, sleep

Lime: Element – Air, Fire; Planet – Sun; Magickal properties – healing, love, protection,

Mace: Element – Air; Planet – Mercury; Magickal properties – clairvoyance, fertility, gain, good luck, love, protection, mental ability, psychic powers

Marjoram: Element – Air; Planet – Venus, Mercury; Magickal properties – animals, cleansing, courage, dreams, grieving, happiness, harmony, health, love, money, peace, prosperity, protection, psychic development, psychic protection, rituals for the dead, success, tranquility, weddings

Mint: Element – Air; Planet – Mercury, Venus; Magickal properties – augment power, exorcism, healing, luck, money, prosperity, protection, sex, strength, travel

Mustard: Element – Fire; Planet – Mars; Magickal properties – binding, commanding, cursing, exorcism, fertility, gain, good luck, health, love, mental ability, passion, protection, sensuality, spell breaking, strength, success

Nutmeg: Element – Fire, Air; Planet – Jupiter; Magickal properties – clairvoyance, divination, dreams, fertility, fidelity, gain, health, love, luck, meditation, money, passion, prosperity, protection, psychic development, rest, sleep

Onion: Element – Fire; Planet – Mars; Magickal properties – clairvoyance, cleansing, contacting other planes, divination, exorcism, healing, lunar rites, magick, prophetic dreams, prosperity, protection, purification, sex, spell breaking

Orange: Element – Fire; Planet – Sun; Magickal properties – divination, harmony, joy, love, luck, money, warmth

Oregano: Element – Air; Planet – Venus; Magickal properties – animals, grieving, happiness, harmony, love, peace, protection, psychic development, tranquility, weddings

Parsley: Element – Earth; Planet – Saturn; Magickal properties – clairvoyance, cleansing, consecration, contacting other planes, divination, fertility, good luck, happiness, invocation, meditation, passion, protection, psychic development, purification, rituals for the dead, sex, speed

Pepper, Black: Element – Fire; Planet – Mars; Magickal properties – binding, exorcism, irritation, lust, protection, strength, warding charms

Peppermint: Element – Air; Planet – Venus; Magickal properties – animals, cleansing, consecration, divination, dreams, endings, energy, exorcism, good luck, grieving, happiness, healing, love, money, passion, prosperity, protection, psychic development, purification, release, renewal, rest, sleep, spirit offering, success, transformation

Pineapple: Element – Fire; Planet – Sun; Magickal properties – chastity, luck, prosperity

Poppy seed: Element – Water; Planet – Moon; Magickal properties – binding, clairvoyance, consecration, cursing, dreams, fertility, prosperity

Potato: Element – Earth; Planet - Moon; Magickal properties – healing

Radish: Element – Fire; Planet – Mars; Magickal properties – protection, sex

Raspberry: Element – Water; Planet – Venus; Magickal properties – love, protection

Rhubarb: Element – Earth; Planet – Venus; Magickal properties – fidelity, protection

Rice: Element – Air; Planet – Sun; Magickal properties – protection, prosperity

Rosemary: Element – Fire; Planet – Sun; Magickal properties – blessings, cleansing, confidence, consecration, courage, dreams, elves, endings, energy, exorcism, fidelity, good luck, grieving, happiness, healing, honesty, inspiration, invocation, knowledge, longevity, love, lunar rites, meditation, memory, mental ability, moon magick, new moon, passion, peace of mind, prevents nightmares, prevents theft, protection, psychic development, psychic protection, purification, release, ritual, rituals for the dead, sea rites, sex, sleep, strength, substitution for any other herb, transformation, water rites, weddings, winter rituals, wisdom, Yule

Saffron: Element – Fire; Planet – Sun; Magickal properties – clairvoyance, cleansing, commanding, consecration, divination, exorcism, happiness, healing, love, magick, psychic development, psychic powers, purification, sex, spell breaking, strength, weather (raises wind)

Sage: Element – Earth; Planet – Mercury, Jupiter; Magickal properties – business, clairvoyance, cleansing, consecration, divination, domestic harmony, energy, happiness, healing, inspiration, keeping secrets, knowledge, longevity, love, Mabon, meditation, money, passion, peace, prosperity, protection, psychic development, psychic protection, purification, retention, Samhain, tranquility, weddings, wisdom, Yule

Savory: Element – Air; Planet – Venus; Magickal properties – animals, attracts males, happiness, love, mediation, mental ability, passion, satyrs, sensuality, virility

Sesame seed: Element – Fire; Planet – Sun; Magickal properties – lust, money, prosperity, sex

Spearmint: Element – Air; Planet – Venus; Magickal properties – animals, consecration, dreams, endings, exorcism, good luck, happiness, healing, love, meditation, mental ability, money, passion, prosperity, protection, psychic development, release, renewal, rest, sleep, spirit offering, success, transformation

Strawberry: Element – Water; Planet – Venus; Magickal properties – love, luck

Tarragon: Element – Fire; Planet – Mercury, Jupiter; Magickal properties – animals, calming, commanding, confidence, courage, keeping secrets, love, passion, peace, prevents theft, protection, retention, sensuality, strength, virility

Thyme: Element – Air; Planet – Venus; Magickal properties – clairvoyance, cleansing, compassion, confidence, consecration, contacting other planes, courage, dreams, exorcism, faeries, grieving, happiness, healing, health, love, magick, meditation, Midsummer, money, passion, prevents nightmares, protection, psychic development, purification, release, renewal, rituals for the dead, sleep, Summer rituals, wishes

Tomato: Element – Water; Planet – Venus; Magickal properties – love, prosperity, protection

Turmeric: Element – Fire; Planet – Mars; Magickal properties – commanding, confidence, courage, exorcism, magick, passion, sensuality, spell breaking, strength

Turnip: Element – Earth; Planet – Moon; Magickal properties – protection

Vanilla: Element – Fire; Planet – Jupiter; Magickal properties – energy, love, lunar rites, new moon, passion, sex

Wintergreen: Element – Earth; Planet – Mercury; Magickal properties – animals, contacting other planes, counteracting hexes, good luck, healing, money, protection

Herbs by Magickal Property

All of the following herbs can be purchased at your local grocery store. Remember that ROSEMARY can be used as a substitute for any herb. Also, the correspondences here are not completely inclusive. There will be many other uses for these herbs that you may discover on your own either through more research or through your own workings.

Animal's: marjoram, oregano, peppermint, savory, spearmint, tarragon, wintergreen

Attract good spirits: catnip

Attracts males: savory

Augment power: mint

Beauty: avocado, catnip, celery seed

Binding: ginger, mustard seed, pepper, poppy seed

Blessings: dill, rosemary

Business: sage

Calming: tarragon

Cat magick: catnip

Celebration: catnip

Chastity: coconut, cucumber, pineapple

Clairvoyance: anise, basil, bay, cinnamon, cloves, coriander/cilantro, garlic, mace, nutmeg, onion, parsley, poppy seed, saffron, sage, thyme

Cleansing: anise, cloves, marjoram, onion, parsley, peppermint, rosemary, saffron, sage, thyme

Commanding: basil, fennel, garlic, mustard seed, pepper, saffron, tarragon, turmeric

Communication: allspice, cinnamon

Compassion: allspice, almond, thyme

Confidence: dill, fennel, garlic, rosemary, tarragon, thyme, turmeric

Consecration: anise, basil, bay, caraway, cinnamon, fennel, garlic, parsley, peppermint, poppy seed, rosemary, saffron, sage, spearmint, thyme

Contacting other planes: anise, onion, parsley, thyme, wintergreen

Counteracting hexes: chili pepper, wintergreen

Courage: basil, fennel, garlic, marjoram, rosemary, tarragon, thyme, turmeric

Death rituals (rites for the dead): basil, marjoram, parsley, rosemary, thyme

Determination: allspice, dill

Divination: anise, basil, bay, celery seeds, cinnamon, cloves, coriander/cilantro, fennel, garlic, nutmeg, onion, orange, parsley, peppermint, saffron, sage, thyme

Domestic harmony: sage

Dreams: bay, dill, marjoram, nutmeg, onion, peppermint, poppy seed, rosemary, spearmint, thyme

Elements: <u>Air</u> – almond, anise, blueberry, caraway, cinnamon, fennel, lemongrass, lime, mace, marjoram, mint, nutmeg, oregano, peppermint, rice, savory, spearmint, thyme; <u>Fire</u> – allspice, basil, bay, black pepper, carrot, chili pepper, chive, cinnamon, cloves, coriander/cilantro, cumin, curry, dill, fennel, flax, garlic, ginger, leek, lime, mustard seed, nutmeg, onion, orange, pineapple, radish, rosemary, saffron, sesame seed, tarragon, turmeric, vanilla <u>Water</u> – apple, avocado, banana, blackberry, cardamom, catnip, coconut, cucumber, grape lemon, lettuce, poppy seed, raspberry, rosemary, strawberry, tomato; <u>Earth</u> – allspice, alum, barley, carrot, celery seed, dill, parsley, potato, rhubarb, sage, turnip, wintergreen

Elves: rosemary

Endings: bay, peppermint, rosemary, spearmint

Energy: allspice, cardamom, cinnamon, fennel, peppermint, rosemary, sage, vanilla

Enhance fertility: cardamom

Envy, stopping: black pepper

Exorcism: basil, bay, black pepper, cloves, cumin, garlic, mint, mustard seed, onion, peppermint, rosemary, saffron, spearmint, thyme, turmeric

Faeries: thyme

Fair Weather: garlic

Fertility: almond, anise, banana, basil, black pepper, caraway, cardamom, carrot, celery seed, coriander/cilantro, cucumber, dill, fennel, grape, mace, mint, mustard seed, nutmeg, parsley, poppy seed,

Fidelity: basil, caraway, chili pepper, cumin, nutmeg, rhubarb, rosemary

Friendship: apple, cloves, lemon

Gain: anise, caraway, coriander/cilantro, dill, fennel, mace, mustard seed, and nutmeg

Good luck: anise, basil, bay, cinnamon, mace, mustard seed, parsley, peppermint, rosemary, spearmint, wintergreen

Gossip, stopping: cloves, garlic

Grieving: basil, marjoram, oregano, peppermint, rosemary, thyme

Happiness: anise, basil, catnip, cinnamon, marjoram, oregano, parsley, peppermint, rosemary, saffron, sage, savory, spearmint, thyme

Harmony: basil, bay, cinnamon, dill, marjoram, orange, oregano, sage

Hatred: basil

Health/healing: allspice, bay, blackberry, caraway seeds, cinnamon, coriander/cilantro, cucumber, fennel, flax, garlic, ginger, lime, marjoram, mint, mustard seed, nutmeg, onion, peppermint, potato, rosemary, saffron, sage, spearmint, thyme, wintergreen

Honesty: basil, caraway, rosemary

Imbolc: basil, bay leaves

Immortality: apple

Initiation: basil

Inspiration: basil, bay, cinnamon, rosemary, sage

Invocation: basil, parsley, rosemary

Joy: orange

Justice: bay

Keeping secrets: caraway, coriander/cilantro, dill, sage, tarragon

Keeps away negative forces: cloves

Knowledge: bay, cinnamon, rosemary, sage

Longevity: cumin, fennel, garlic, lemon, rosemary, sage

Love: anise, apple, avocado, barley, basil, bay, caraway, cardamom, catnip, celery seed, chili pepper, cinnamon, cloves, coriander/cilantro, cumin, dill, fennel, ginger, lemon, lime, mace, marjoram, mustard seed, nutmeg, orange, oregano, peppermint, raspberry, rosemary, saffron, sage, savory, spearmint, strawberry, tarragon, thyme, tomato, vanilla

Luck: allspice, anise, basil, bay leaves, catnip, cinnamon, mace, mint, mustard, nutmeg, orange, parsley, peppermint, pineapple, rosemary, spearmint, strawberry, wintergreen

Lunar rites: onion, rosemary, vanilla

Lust: black pepper, lemongrass, sesame seed

Mabon: sage

Magick: bay, garlic, onion, saffron, thyme, turmeric

Meditation: cinnamon, fennel, nutmeg, parsley, rosemary, sage, thyme, savory, spearmint

Memory: bay, caraway, cloves, rosemary

Mental Ability: caraway seeds, celery seed, grape, mace, mustard, rosemary, savory, spearmint

Midsummer: fennel, thyme

Money: allspice, almond, anise, basil, bay, cinnamon, cloves, dill, fennel, garlic, marjoram, mint, nutmeg, orange, peppermint, sage, sesame seed, spearmint, thyme, wintergreen

Moon magick: lemon, rosemary

New moon: rosemary, vanilla

Nightmares, preventing: anise, garlic, rosemary, thyme

Opposition, overcoming: bay, garlic

Passion: anise, basil, bay, black pepper, caraway, celery seed, cinnamon, cloves, coriander/cilantro, dill, garlic, ginger, mustard seed, nutmeg, parsley, peppermint, rosemary, sage, savory, spearmint, tarragon, thyme, turmeric, vanilla

Peace: basil, bay, cinnamon, coriander/cilantro, cumin, dill, marjoram, oregano, sage, tarragon

Peace of mind: caraway, cloves, rosemary

Planets: <u>Sun</u> - bay, cinnamon, cloves, lime, orange, pineapple, rice, rosemary, saffron, sesame seed, ; <u>Moon</u> – coconut, cucumber, grape, lemon, lettuce, poppy seed, potato, turnip; <u>Mercury</u> – almond, anise, caraway, celery seed, cinnamon, dill, fennel, flax, lemon grass, mace, marjoram, mint, sage, tarragon, wintergreen; <u>Venus</u> - allspice, almond, apple, avocado, banana, barley, blackberry, cardamom, catnip, marjoram, mint, oregano, peppermint, raspberry, rhubarb, savory, spearmint, strawberry, thyme, tomato; <u>Mars</u> – allspice, basil, black pepper, cardamom, carrot, chili pepper, chive, cinnamon, coriander, cumin, curry, garlic, ginger, leek, mustard seed, onion, radish, turmeric; <u>Jupiter</u> -

anise, avocado, blueberry, cloves, nutmeg, sage, tarragon, vanilla; <u>Saturn</u> – alum, celery seed, parsley

Power: ginger

Prevent theft: basil, caraway seeds, dill weed, rosemary, tarragon

Prevent nightmares: anise, garlic, rosemary, thyme

Prophetic dreams: onion

Prosperity: allspice, almond, banana, basil, blackberry, cinnamon, cloves, dill weed, flax, ginger, grape, marjoram, mint, nutmeg, onion, peppermint, pineapple, poppy seed, rice, sage, sesame seed, spearmint, tomato

Protection: alum, anise, barley, basil, bay, blackberry, black pepper, blueberry, caraway, cinnamon, cloves, coconut, coriander/cilantro, cumin, curry, dill, fennel, flax, garlic, leek, lettuce, lime, mace, marjoram, mint, mustard seed, nutmeg, onion, oregano, parsley, peppermint, radish, raspberry, rhubarb, rice, rosemary, sage, spearmint, tarragon, thyme, tomato, turnip, wintergreen

Protection against disease: chive

Protection from evil: alum, chive, curry

Protection of ones home: cumin

Psychic development: anise, basil, bay, celery seed, cinnamon, cloves, ginger, marjoram, nutmeg, oregano, parsley, peppermint, rosemary, saffron, sage, spearmint, thyme

Psychic powers: flax, lemongrass, mace, saffron

Psychic protection: anise, basil, bay, cloves, dill, fennel, ginger, marjoram, rosemary, sage

Purification: anise, basil, bay, cinnamon, cloves, coconut, fennel, garlic, lemon, onion, parsley, peppermint, rosemary, saffron, sage, thyme

Release: bay, cloves, peppermint, rosemary, spearmint, thyme

Renewal: peppermint, spearmint, thyme

Repel evil at night: curry

Repel snakes: lemongrass

Rest: dill, nutmeg, peppermint, spearmint

Retention: caraway, coriander/cilantro, dill, sage, tarragon

Rituals for the dead: basil, marjoram, parsley, rosemary, thyme

Samhain: sage

Satyr's: savory

Sea/water rituals: rosemary

Sensuality: caraway, ginger, mustard seed, savory, tarragon, turmeric

Sex: avocado, caraway seeds, cardamom, carrot, celery seed, cinnamon, dill weed, garlic, lemongrass, mint, onion, parsley, radish, rosemary, saffron, sesame seed, vanilla

Sexual energy: cardamom

Sleep: dill, lettuce, nutmeg, peppermint, rosemary, spearmint, thyme

Spell-breaking: basil, bay, cloves, garlic, mustard seed, onion, saffron, turmeric

Spirit offering: peppermint, spearmint

Spirituality: cinnamon

Strength: basil, bay, black pepper, fennel, garlic, mint, mustard seed, rosemary, saffron, tarragon, turmeric

Substitution for any other herb: rosemary

Success basil, bay, cinnamon, garlic, ginger, marjoram, mustard seed, peppermint, spearmint

Summer rituals (Spring Equinox through Fall Equinox): fennel, thyme

Theft, preventing: basil, caraway, dill, rosemary, tarragon

Tranquility: basil, bay, cinnamon, dill, marjoram, oregano, sage

Transformation: bay, peppermint, rosemary, spearmint

Travel: mint

Virility: fennel, savory, tarragon

Warding: black pepper

Warmth: orange

Water rites: rosemary

Weather: garlic (fair), saffron (raise wind)

Weddings: anise, caraway, coriander/cilantro, marjoram, oregano, rosemary, sage

Winter rituals (Fall Equinox through Spring Equinox): basil, bay, rosemary, sage

Wisdom: almond, bay, cinnamon, rosemary, sage

Wishes: bay, thyme

Yule: bay leaves, rosemary, sage

Magickal Days

When planning magickal workings, consideration needs to be given as to when the work needs to be performed for best effect. You need to decide the best time or day for when to perform it.

Days have their own magickal associations, which are similar to and connected with the other tables - Candles, Color and Incense. Thus they create harmony while generating power, when all are working together. If you are unable to do your spell work on the associated day, that is okay, it just adds a boost if you can.

Sunday: Is associated with the Sun and the colors of - Yellow, Gold and Orange

Sunday is the best time to deal with such matters as: Achievement, Advancement, Ambition, Authority, Buying, Careers Goals, Children, Crops, Divination, Drama, Fairs, Figures, Fun, Healing Energy, Health, Law, Men's Mysteries, Personnel Finances, Physical Strength, Promotion, Selling, Speculation, Success, Totem Animals, Volunteer and Civic Services

Monday: Is associated with the Moon and the colors of - White, Silver, Grey and Pearl

Monday is the best time to deal with such matters as: Antiques, Archetypes, Astral Travel, Astrology, Bodies of Water, Children, Domestic Concerns, Dreams, Emotions, Fluids, Full moon magic, Household Activities, Imagination, Initiation, Justice, Magick, Meditation, New-Age Pursuits, Nursing, Peace, Protection, Psychic Pursuits, Psychology, Public, Purity, Reincarnation, Religious Experiences, Shape-shifting, Short Trips, Sincerity, Spirituality, Totem Animals, Trip Planning, Truth, Warding off Doubts and Fears, Water, Women, Women's Mysteries

Tuesday: Is associated with Mars and the colors of - Red, Pink and Orange

Tuesday is the best time to deal with such matters as: Action, Aggression, Business, Buying and Selling Animals, Combat, Confrontation, Courage, Cutting, Energy, Gardening, Guns, Hunting, Mechanical Things, Metals, Muscular Activity, New Beginnings, Partnerships, Passion, Physical Energy, Police, Repairs, Sex, Soldiers, Sports, Strife, Surgery, Swift Movement, Tools, Woodworking

Wednesday: Is associated with Mercury and the colors of Purple, Magenta and Silver

Wednesday is the best time to deal with such matters as: Accounting, Advertising, Astrology, Clerks, Communication, Computers, Correspondence, Critics, Editing, Editors, Education, Healing, Hiring Employees, Intelligence, Journalists, Kin, Learning Languages, Legal Appointments, Memory, Merchants, Messages, Music, Neighbors, Phone Calls, Placing Ads, Siblings, Signing Contracts, Students, Visiting Friends, Visual Arts, Wisdom, and Writing

Thursday: Is associated with Jupiter and the colors of - Blue and Metallic Colors

Thursday is the best time to deal with such matters as: Broadcasting, Business, Charity, College Education, Correspondence Courses, Doctors, Expansion, Forecasting, Foreign Interests, Gambling, Growth, Guardians, Horses, Logic, Long Distance Travel, Luck, Material Wealth, Merchants, Philosophy, Political Power, Psychologists, Publicity, Publishing, Reading, Religion, Researching, Self-improvement, Social Matters, Sports, Studying, and The Law

Friday: Is associated with Venus and the colors of - Green, Pink and White

Friday is the best time to deal with such matters as: Affection, Alliances, Architects, Artistic Ability, Artists, Balance, Beauticians, Beauty, Change, Chiropractors, Cosmetics, Courage, Courtship, Dancers, Dating, Decorating, Designers, Engineers, Entertainers, Fashion, Fertility, Friendship, Gardening, Gifts, Grace, Harmony, Herbal Magick, Household Improvements, Income, Luck, Luxury, Marriage, Material Things, Music, Painting, Partners, Peace, Physical Healing, Planning Parties, Poetry, Prosperity, Relationships, Romantic Love, Shopping, Social Activity, Soul-mates, Success

Saturday: Is associated with Saturn and the colors of - Black, Grey, Red and White

Saturday is the best time to deal with such matters as: Binding, Bones, Civil Servants, Criminals, Death, Debts, Dentists, Discoveries, Farm Workers, Financing, Handwork, Joint Money Matters, Justice, Karma, Laws of society, Limits, Manifestation, Material Gain, Math's, Murderers, Neutralization, Obstacles, Patience, Plumbing, Protection, Real Estate, Real Estate, Reality, Relations with Older People, Sacrifice, Separation, Stability, Stalkers, Structure's, Teeth, Tests, Transformation, Wills

Magickal Days by Magickal Property

When planning magickal workings, consideration needs to be given as to when the work needs to be performed for best effect. You need to decide the best time or day for when to perform it.

Days have their own magickal associations, which are similar to and connected with the other tables - Candles, Color and Incense. Thus they create harmony while generating power, when all are working together. If you are unable to do your spell work on the associated day, that is okay, it just adds a boost if you can.

Accounting: Wednesday

Achievement: Sunday

Action: Tuesday

Advancement: Sunday

Advertising: Wednesday

Affection: Friday

Aggression: Tuesday

Alliances: Friday

Ambition: Sunday

Antiques: Monday

Archetypes: Monday

Architects: Friday

Artistic Ability: Friday

Artists: Friday

Astral Travel: Monday

Astrology: Monday, Wednesday

Authority: Sunday

Balance: Friday

Beauticians: Friday

Beauty: Friday

Binding: Saturday

Black: Saturday

Blue: Thursday

Bodies of Water: Monday

Bones: Saturday

Broadcasting: Thursday

Business: Tuesday

Business: Thursday

Buying and Selling Animals: Tuesday

Buying: Sunday

Career Goals: Sunday

Change: Friday

Charity: Thursday

Children: Sunday, Monday

Chiropractors: Friday

Civil Servants: Saturday

Clerks: Wednesday

College Education: Thursday

Combat: Tuesday

Communication: Wednesday

Computers: Wednesday

Confrontation: Tuesday

Correspondence Courses: Thursday

Correspondence: Wednesday

Cosmetics: Friday

Courage: Tuesday

Courage: Friday

Courtship: Friday

Criminals: Saturday

Critics: Wednesday

Crops: Sunday

Cutting: Tuesday

Dancers: Friday

Dating: Friday

Death: Saturday

Debts: Saturday

Decorating: Friday

Dentists: Saturday

Designers: Friday

Discoveries: Saturday

Divination: Sunday

Doctors: Thursday

Domestic Concerns: Monday

Drama: Sunday

Dreams: Monday

Editing: Wednesday

Editors: Wednesday

Education: Wednesday

Emotions: Monday

Energy: Tuesday

Engineers: Friday

Entertainers: Friday

Expansion: Thursday

Fairs: Sunday

Farm Workers: Saturday

Fashion: Friday

Fertility: Friday

Figures: Sunday

Financing: Saturday

Fluids: Monday

Forecasting: Thursday

Foreign Interests: Thursday

Friendship: Friday

Full Moon Magick: Monday

Fun: Sunday

Gambling: Thursday

Gardening: Tuesday, Friday

Gifts: Friday

Gold: Sunday

Grace: Friday

Green: Friday

Grey: Monday, Saturday

Growth: Thursday

Guardians: Thursday

Guns: Tuesday

Handwork: Saturday

Harmony: Friday

Healing Energy: Sunday

Healing: Wednesday

Health: Sunday

Herbal Magick: Friday

Hiring Employees: Wednesday

Horses: Thursday

Household Activities: Monday

Household Improvements: Friday

Hunting: Tuesday

Imagination: Monday

Income: Friday

Initiation: Monday

Intelligence: Wednesday

Joint Money Matters: Saturday

Journalists: Wednesday

Jupiter: Thursday

Justice: Monday, Saturday

Karma: Saturday

Kin: Wednesday

Law: Sunday

Laws of society: Saturday

Learning Languages: Wednesday

Legal Appointments: Wednesday

Limits: Saturday

Logic: Thursday

Long Distance Travel: Thursday

Luck: Thursday

Luck: Friday

Luxury: Friday

Magenta: Wednesday

Magick: Monday

Manifestation: Saturday

Marriage: Friday

Mars: Tuesday

Material Gain: Saturday

Material Things: Friday

Material Wealth: Thursday

Math's: Saturday

Mechanical Things: Tuesday

Meditation: Monday

Memory: Wednesday

Men's Mysteries: Sunday

Merchants: Wednesday, Thursday

Mercury: Wednesday

Messages: Wednesday

Metallic Colors: Thursday

Metals: Tuesday

Moon: Monday

Murderers: Saturday

Muscular Activity: Tuesday

Music: Wednesday

Music: Friday

Neighbors: Wednesday

Neutralization: Saturday

New Beginnings: Tuesday

New-Age Pursuits: Monday

Nursing: Monday

Obstacles: Saturday

Orange: Sunday, Tuesday

Painting: Friday

Partners: Friday

Partnerships: Tuesday

Passion: Tuesday

Patience: Saturday

Peace: Monday, Friday

Pearl: Monday

Personal Finances: Sunday

Philosophy: Thursday

Phone Calls: Wednesday

Physical Energy: Tuesday

Physical Healing: Friday

Physical Strength: Sunday

Pink: Friday, Tuesday

Placing Ads: Wednesday

Planning Parties: Friday

Plumbing: Saturday

Poetry: Friday

Police: Tuesday

Political Power: Thursday

Promotion: Sunday

Prosperity: Friday

Protection: Monday, Saturday

Psychic Pursuits: Monday

Psychologists: Thursday

Psychology: Monday

Public: Monday

Publicity: Thursday

Publishing: Thursday

Purity: Monday

Purple: Wednesday

Reading: Thursday

Real Estate: Saturday

Reality: Saturday

Red: Saturday, Tuesday

Reincarnation: Monday

Relations with Older People: Saturday

Relationships: Friday

Religion: Thursday

Religious Experiences: Monday

Repairs: Tuesday

Researching: Thursday

Romantic Love: Friday

Sacrifice: Saturday

Saturn: Saturday

Self-improvement: Thursday

Selling: Sunday

Separation: Saturday

Sex: Tuesday

Shape-shifting: Monday

Shopping: Friday

Short Trips: Monday

Siblings: Wednesday

Signing Contracts: Wednesday

Silver: Monday, Wednesday

Sincerity: Monday

Social Activity: Friday

Social Matters: Thursday

Soldiers: Tuesday

Soul-mates: Friday

Speculation: Sunday

Spirituality: Monday

Sports: Tuesday

Sports: Thursday

Stability: Saturday

Stalkers: Saturday

Strife: Tuesday

Structure's: Saturday

Students: Wednesday

Studying: Thursday

Success: Sunday, Friday

Sun: Sunday

Surgery: Tuesday

Swift Movement: Tuesday

Teeth: Saturday

Tests: Saturday

The Law: Thursday

Tools: Tuesday

Totem Animals: Sunday, Monday

Transformation: Saturday

Trip Planning: Monday

Truth: Monday

Venus: Friday

Visiting Friends: Wednesday

Visual Arts: Wednesday

Volunteer and Civic Services: Sunday

Warding off Doubts and Fears: Monday

Water: Monday

White: Friday, Monday, Saturday

Wills: Saturday

Wisdom: Wednesday

Women: Monday

Women's Mysteries: Monday

Woodworking: Tuesday

Writing: Wednesday

Yellow: Sunday

Resins

Resins are a little more difficult to find than herbs or flowers and even incense. You will likely have to purchase these online or from a new age store in your local area. These resins listed here are not the exhaustive list; they are the ones that I have used most often in my workings. Please use this list as a basis for your research on other resins. You may find that some of these resins will do things for you that I have not listed here, that is perfectly fine.

Aloes: Element – Water; Planet – Moon, Venus; Magickal Properties – Guard against evil influences, luck, prevent household accidents, prevents feelings of loneliness, protection, success

Asafoetida: Element – Fire; Planet – Mars; Magickal properties – Exorcism, increases the power of any ritual, protection, purification

Balm of Gilead: Element – Water; Planet – Venus; Magickal properties – Healing, love, manifestations, protection, healing

Benzoin: Element – Air; Planet – Sun; Magickal properties – Astral travel, base for incense, enhance concentration, focus, promotes generosity, prosperity, protects spirit while travelling, purification

Camphor: Element – Water; Planet – Moon; Magickal properties – Chastity, divination, health

Copal: Element – Fire; Planet – Sun; Magickal properties – Love, purification

Dragon's Blood: Element – Fire; Planet – Mars; Magickal properties – Exorcism, love, potency, protection

Frankincense: Element – Fire; Planet – Sun; Magickal properties – Exorcism, protection, spirituality, substitute for any other resin

Gum Arabic: Element – Air; Planet – Sun; Magickal properties – Purifies evil, purify negativity

Mastic: Element – Air; Planet – Sun; Magickal properties – Lust, manifestations, psychic powers

Myrrh: Element – Water; Planet – Moon; Magickal properties – Exorcism, healing, protection, spirituality

Pine: Element – Air; Planet – Mars; Magickal properties – Exorcism, fertility, healing, money, protection

Resins by Magickal Property

Resins are a little more difficult to find than herbs or flowers and even incense. You will likely have to purchase these online or from a new age store in your local area. These resins listed here are not the exhaustive list; they are the ones that I have used most often in my workings. Please use this list as a basis for your research on other resins. You may find that some of these resins will do things for you that I have not listed here, that is perfectly fine.

Astral travel: Benzoin

Base for incense: Benzoin

Chastity: Camphor

Divination: Camphor

Element: Air – Benzoin, gum arabic, mastic, pine; Fire – Asafoetida, copal, dragon's blood, frankincense; Water – aloes, balm of gilead, camphor, myrrh

Enhance concentration: Benzoin

Exorcism: asafoetida, dragon's blood, frankincense, myrrh, pine

Fertility: pine

Focus: benzoin

Generosity: benzoin

Guard against evil influences: aloes

Healing: Balm of gilead, myrrh, pine

Health: camphor

Increases the power of any ritual: asafoetida

Love: Balm of gilead, camphor, dragon's blood

Luck: aloes

Lust: mastic

Manifestations: Balm of gilead, mastic

Money: pine

Planet: Mars – asafoetida, dragon's blood, pine; Moon – Aloes, camphor, myrrh, ; Sun – Benzoin, copal, frankincense, gum arabic, mastic; Venus – aloes, balm of gilead

Potency: potency

Prevent household accidents: aloes

Prevents feelings of loneliness: aloes

Promotes generosity: benzoin

Prosperity: benzoin,

Protection: aloes, asafoetida, balm of Gilead, dragon's blood, frankincense, myrrh, pine

Protects spirit while travelling: benzoin,

Psychic powers: mastic

Purification: asafoetida, benzoin, camphor

Purify evil: gum arabic,

Purify negativity: gum arabic

Spirituality: frankincense, myrrh,

Substitute for any other resin: frankincense

Success: aloes

Tincturing Herbs
Remember that the following list is not all inclusive. It is meant as a starting point for your research of herbs that can be used in tinctures. Research herbs and experiment to see if you can find other herbs not listed here or different results from the herbs that are listed here. The herbs that I have listed here you should

be able to find in the spice section of your local grocery store. The resins you will likely have to purchase from a new age shop in your area or online. Herbs will be marked with an (H) and resins will be marked with an (R).

Benzoin (R): increase business success, purification, sharpen mental powers

Camphor (R): full moon baths, healing amulets, lessen sexual desire

Cinnamon (H): money, protection, psychic powers

Clove (H): exorcism, love, money, protection

Copal (R): protection, spirituality

Frankincense (R): exorcism, great for use with incense papers, luck, protection, purification, spirituality

Myrrh (R): great for use with incense papers, healing, protection, and spirituality

Nutmeg (H): health, luck, money, psychic powers

Peppermint (H): *This is a slow brewing herb* love, money, purification, sleep

Rosemary (H): Substitute for any other needed tincture

Sage (H): healing, protection, purification, wisdom, wishing

Star Anise (H): improve psychic awareness

Vanilla (H): attract love, promote physical energy, and stimulate mental processes

Tincturing Herbs by Magickal Property
  Remember that the following list is not all inclusive. It is meant as a starting point for your research of herbs that can be used in tinctures. Research herbs and experiment to see if you can find other herbs not listed here or different results from the herbs that are listed here. The herbs that I have listed here you should

be able to find in the spice section of your local grocery store. The resins you will likely have to purchase from a new age shop in your area or online. Herbs will be marked with an (H) and resins will be marked with an (R).

Attract love: vanilla (H)

Exorcism: clove (H), frankincense (R)

Full moon baths: camphor (R)

Great for use with incense papers: frankincense (R), myrrh (R)

Healing amulets: camphor (R)

Healing: myrrh (R), sage (H)

Health: nutmeg (H)

Improve psychic awareness: star anise (H)

Increase business success: benzoin (R)

Lessen sexual desire: camphor (R)

Love: clove (H), peppermint (H)

Luck: frankincense (R), nutmeg (H)

Money: cinnamon (H), clove (H), nutmeg (H), peppermint (H)

Promote physical energy: vanilla (H)

Protection: cinnamon (H), clove (H), copal (R), frankincense (R), myrrh (R), sage (H)

Psychic powers: cinnamon (H), nutmeg (H)

Purification: benzoin (R), frankincense (R), peppermint (H), sage (H)

Sharpen mental powers: benzoin (R)

Sleep: peppermint (H)

Spirituality: copal (R), frankincense (R), myrrh (R)

Stimulate mental processes: vanilla (H)

Substitute for any other needed tincture: rosemary (H)

Wisdom: sage (H)

Wishing: sage (H)

Woods

The woods that are listed here will not be found in everyone's area that reads this book and they may not be readily available. This list is also not exhaustive; it is merely a starting point. If one of the woods listed here is indigenous to your area, you can use the bark from that tree in your magickal workings. Each wood listed will have its element, planetary and magickal correspondences. You may find that a tree has a different effect on your magickal workings, and that is fine. The correspondences that I have listed here are those that I have discovered through my own use of that particular wood. Use this list as a starting point for your research on the various types of woods that are available in your area. Should you decide to use any of the woods listed here, or any that are not listed here, remember to always ask the permission of the tree you are collecting bark from.

Alder: Element – Fire, Water; Planet – Neptune; Magickal properties – Imbolc, resurrection

Apple: Element – Water; Planet – Venus; Magickal properties – beauty, healing, love, regeneration

Apricot: Element – Water; Planet – Venus; Magickal properties – love

Ash: Element – Fire; Planet – Sun; Magickal properties – balance, communication, focus, healing, intelligence, spiritual health, wisdom

Aspen: Element – Air; Planet – Mercury; Magickal properties – communication, intuition, overcome obstacles

Bay: Element – Fire; Planet – Sun; Magickal properties – clairvoyance, healing, love, protection, purification, romance, strength

Beech: Element – Water; Planet – Saturn; Magickal properties – gain insight, guidance from past

Birch: Element – Water; Planet – Venus; Magickal properties – fertility, healing, new beginnings, purification, vitality

Cedar: Element – Fire; Planet – Sun; Magickal properties – cleansing, create sacred space, longevity, preservation, protection

Cherry: Element – Water; Planet – Venus; Magickal properties – divination, focus, healing, intuition, love, overcome obstacles, stability

Chestnut: Element – Fire; Planet – Jupiter; Magickal properties – love

Cypress: Element – Water; Planet – Saturn; Magickal properties – easing losses, healing, protection

Dogwood: Element – Air; Planet – Sun; Magickal properties – protection, wishes

Ebony: Element – Fire; Planet – Sun; Magickal properties – power, protection

Elder: Element – Water; Planet – Venus; Magickal properties – beginnings, do not burn, endings

Elm: Element – Water; Planet – Saturn; Magickal properties – grounding, stability

Eucalyptus: Element – Water; Planet – Moon; Magickal properties – healing, protection

Fir: Element – Fire; Planet – Jupiter; Magickal properties – birth, power, prosperity, rebirth

Hawthorn: Element – Fire; Planet – Mars; Magickal properties – love, marriage, pleasure, protection, purity, stimulation

Hazel: Element – Air; Planet – Sun; Magickal properties – creativity, inspiration, knowledge, wisdom

Holly: Element – Fire; Planet – Mars; Magickal properties – balance, ease the passage of death, rest, sleep, Yule

Juniper: Element – Fire; Planet – Sun; Magickal properties – protection

Lemon: Element – Water; Planet – Moon; Magickal properties – chastity, divination, healing, neutrality

Lime: Element – Fire; Planet – Sun; Magickal properties – healing, love, protection

Magnolia: Element – Earth; Planet – Venus; Magickal properties – fidelity

Maple: Element – Air; Planet – Jupiter; Magickal properties – abundance, art, beauty, binding, communication, knowledge, success

Mimosa: Element – Water; Planet – Saturn; Magickal properties – love, prophetic dreams, protection, purification

Mulberry: Element – Air; Planet – Mercury; Magickal properties – protection, strength

Myrtle: Element – Water; Planet – Venus; Magickal properties – fertility, love, money, peace, youth

Oak: Element – Fire; Planet – Sun; Magickal properties – balance, courage, fertility, protection, solidity, strength, success, truth

Olive: Element – Fire; Planet – Sun; Magickal properties – fidelity, marriage, money, peace, security

Orange: Element – Fire; Planet – Sun; Magickal properties – love, marriage

Peach: Element – Water; Planet – Venus; Magickal properties – exorcism, fertility, longevity, love, wishes

Pear: Element – Water; Planet – Venus; Magickal properties – love, lust

Pecan: Element – Air; Planet – Mercury; Magickal properties – employment, money

Persimmon: Element – Water; Planet – Venus; Magickal properties – healing, luck

Pine: Element – Air; Planet – Mars; Magickal properties – fertility, fortune, guilt, health, personal issues, prosperity

Pistachio: Element – Air; Planet – Mercury; Magickal properties – breaking love spells

Plum: Element – Water; Planet – Venus; Magickal properties – healing

Pomegranate: Element – Air; Planet – Mercury; Magickal properties – divination, fertility, luck, Wealth, wishes

Poplar: Element – Water; Planet – Saturn; Magickal properties – communication, resistance, shielding

Prickly ash: Element – Fire; Planet – Mars; Magickal properties – love

Rowan: Element – Fire; Planet – Sun; Magickal properties – banishing, invoke spirits, protection

Sagebrush: Element – Earth; Planet – Venus; Magickal properties – exorcism, purification

Sandalwood: Element – Water; Planet – Moon; Magickal properties – exorcism, healing, protection, spirituality

Sassafras: Element – Fire; Planet – Jupiter; Magickal properties – drive away evil, ease digestion, prosperity, rest, sleep

Slippery elm: Element – Air; Planet – Saturn; Magickal properties – end gossip

Walnut: Element – Fire; Planet – Sun; Magickal properties – adjustment to change, intuition

Willow: Element – Water; Planet – Moon; Magickal properties – crone energy, intuition, moon magick, psychic power

Witch Hazel: Element – Fire; Planet – Sun; Magickal properties – chastity, protection

Yew: Element – Earth, Water; Planet – Saturn; Magickal properties – do not burn, immortality, psychic awareness, transformation

Woods by Magickal Property

The woods that are listed here will not be found in everyone's area that reads this book and they may not be readily available. This list is also not exhaustive; it is merely a starting point. If one of the woods listed here is indigenous to your area, you can use the bark from that tree in your magickal workings. Each wood listed will have its element, planetary and magickal correspondences. You may find that a tree has a different effect on your magickal workings, and that is fine. The correspondences that I have listed here are those that I have discovered through my own use of that particular wood. Use this list as a starting point for your research on the various types of woods that are available in your area. Should you decide to use any of the woods listed here, or any that are not listed here, remember to always ask the permission of the tree you are collecting bark from.

Abundance: maple

Adjustment to change: walnut

Air: aspen, dogwood, hazel, maple, mulberry, pecan, pine, pistachio, pomegranate, slippery elm

Art: maple

Balance: ash, holly, oak

Banishing: rowan

Beauty: apple, maple

Beginnings: elder

Binding: maple

Birth: fir

Breaking love spells: pistachio

Chastity: lemon, witch hazel

Clairvoyance: bay

Cleansing: cedar

Communication: ash, aspen, maple, poplar

Courage: oak

Create sacred space: cedar

Creativity: hazel

Crone energy: willow

Divination: cherry, lemon, pomegranate

Do not burn: elder, yew

Drive away evil: sassafras

Earth: magnolia, sagebrush, yew

Ease digestion: sassafras

Ease the passage of death: holly

Easing losses: cypress

Employment: pecan

End gossip: slippery elm

Endings: elder

Exorcism: peach, sagebrush, sandalwood

Fertility: birch, myrtle, oak, peach, pine, pomegranate

Fidelity: magnolia, olive

Fire: alder, ash, bay, cedar, chestnut, ebony, fir, hawthorn, holly, juniper, lime, oak, olive, orange, prickly ash, rowan, sassafras, walnut, witch hazel

Focus: ash, cherry

Fortune: pine

Gain insight: beech

Grounding: elm

Guidance: beech

Guilt: pine

Healing: apple, ash, bay, birch, cherry, cypress, eucalyptus, lemon, lime, persimmon, plum, sandalwood

Health: pine

Imbolc: alder

Immortality: yew

Inspiration: hazel

Intelligence: ash

Intuition: aspen, cherry, walnut, willow

Invoke Spirits: rowan

Jupiter: chestnut, fir, maple, sassafras

Knowledge: hazel, maple

Longevity: cedar, peach

Love: apple, apricot, bay, cherry, chestnut, hawthorn, lime, mimosa, myrtle, orange, peach, pear, prickly ash

Luck: persimmon, pomegranate

Lust: pear

Marriage: hawthorn, olive, orange

Mars: hawthorn, holly, pine, prickly ash

Mercury: aspen, mulberry pecan, pistachio, pomegranate

Money: myrtle, olive, pecan

Moon: eucalyptus, lemon, sandalwood, willow

Moon magick: willow

Neptune: alder

Neutrality: lemon

New beginnings: birch

Overcome obstacles: aspen, cherry

Peace: myrtle, olive

Personal issues: pine

Pleasure: hawthorn

Power: ebony, fir

Preservation: cedar

Prophetic dreams: mimosa

Prosperity: fir, pine, sassafras

Protection: bay, cedar, cypress, dogwood, ebony, eucalyptus, hawthorn, juniper, lime, mimosa, mulberry, oak, rowan, sandalwood, witch hazel

Psychic awareness: yew

Psychic power: willow

Purification: bay, birch, mimosa, sagebrush

Purity: hawthorn

Rebirth: fir

Regeneration: apple

Resistance: poplar

Rest: holly, sassafras

Resurrection: alder

Romance: bay

Saturn: beech, cypress, elm, mimosa, poplar, slippery elm, yew

Security: olive

Shielding: poplar

Sleep: holly, sassafras

Solidity: oak

Spiritual health: ash

Spirituality: sandalwood

Stability: cherry, elm

Stimulation: hawthorn

Strength: bay, mulberry, oak

Success: maple, oak

Sun: ash, bay, cedar, dogwood, ebony, hazel, juniper, lime, oak, olive, orange, rowan, walnut, witch hazel

Transformation: yew

Truth: oak

Venus: apple, apricot, birch, cherry, elder, magnolia, myrtle, peach, pear, persimmon, plum, sagebrush

Vitality: birch

Water: apple, apricot, beech, birch, cherry, cypress, elder, elm, eucalyptus, lemon, mimosa, myrtle, peach, pear, persimmon, plum, poplar, sandalwood, willow, yew

Wealth: pomegranate

Wisdom: ash, hazel

Wishes: dogwood, peach, pomegranate

Youth: myrtle

Yule: holly

Sacred Texts

There are many texts that Witches will call sacred. I am not going to list them all here as that could be a book all by itself. What I am going to list here are the ones that I have in my personal Book of Shadows. If you would like to find more texts than what I have included here, you can easily search the internet for Pagan Sacred Texts, Witchcraft Sacred Texts, Wiccan Sacred Texts, etc.

The first of the sacred texts that I am going to include is the "13 Principles of Wiccan Belief" which was written in 1973 by the Council of American Witches. These beliefs are a part of the United States Army Chaplain Handbook.

The 13 Principles of Wiccan Belief

1. We practice rites to attune ourselves with the natural rhythm of life forces marked by the phases of the Moon and the seasonal Quarters and Cross Quarters.
2. We recognize that our intelligence gives us a unique responsibility toward our environment. We seek to live in harmony with nature in ecological balance offering fulfillment to life and consciousness within an evolutionary concept.
3. We acknowledge a depth of power far greater than that apparent to the average person. Because it is far greater than ordinary it is sometimes called 'supernatural', but we see it as lying within that which is naturally potential to all.
4. We conceive of the Creative Power in the universe as manifesting through polarity – as masculine and feminine – and that this same Creative Power lies in all people and functions through the interaction of the masculine and the feminine. We value neither above the other knowing each to be

supportive of the other. We value sex as pleasure as the symbol and embodiment of life, and as one of the sources of energy used in magical practice and religious worship.

5. We recognize both outer worlds and inner, or psychological worlds sometimes known as the Spiritual World, the Collective Unconsciousness, the Inner Planes etc. – and we see in the interaction of these two dimensions the basis for paranormal phenomena and magical exercises. We neglect neither dimension for the other, seeing both as necessary for our fulfillment.

6. We do not recognize any authoritarian hierarchy, but do honor those who teach, respect those who share their greater knowledge and wisdom, and acknowledge those who have courageously given of themselves in leadership.

7. We see religion, magick and wisdom in living as being united in the way one views the world and lives within it – a world view and philosophy of life which we identify as Witchcraft – the Wiccan Way.

8. Calling oneself 'Witch' does not make a Witch – but neither does heredity itself, nor the collecting of titles, degrees and initiations. A Witch seek to control the forces within her/himself that make life possible in order to live wisely and without harm to others and in harmony with nature.

9. We believe in the affirmation and fulfillment of life in a continuation of evolution and development of consciousness giving meaning to the Universe we know and our personal role within it.

10. Our only animosity towards Christianity, or towards any other religion or philosophy of life, is to the extent that its institutions have claimed to be 'the only way' and have sought to deny freedom to others and to suppress other ways of religious practice and belief.

11. As American Witches, we are not threatened by debates on the history of the craft, the origins of various terms, the legitimacy of various aspects of different traditions. We are concerned with our present and our future.

12. We do not accept the concept of absolute evil, nor do we worship any entity known as 'Satan' or 'the Devil' as defined by Christian tradition. We do not seek power through the suffering of others, nor accept that personal benefit can be derived only by denial to another.

13. We believe that we should seek within Nature that which is contributory to our health and well-being.

The next sacred text I am going to include is The Witches Creed which was written by Doreen Valiente and was published in the book "Witchcraft for Tomorrow" on pages 172-173.

The Witches' Creed
Doreen Valiente

Hear Now the words of the witches,
The secrets we hid in the night,
When dark was our destiny's pathway,
That now we bring forth into light.

Mysterious water and fire,
The earth and the wide-ranging air,
By hidden quintessence we know them,
And will and keep silent and dare.

The birth and rebirth of all nature,
The passing of winter and spring,
We share with the life universal,
Rejoice in the magical ring.

Four times in the year the Great Sabbat
Returns, and the witches are seen
At Lammas and Candlemas dancing,
On May Eve and old Hallowe'en.

When day-time and night-time are equal,
When sun is at greatest and least,
The four Lesser Sabbats are summoned,
And Witches gather in feast.

Thirteen silver moons in a year are,
Thirteen is the coven's array.
Thirteen times at Esbat make merry,
For each golden year and a day.

The power that was passed down the age,
Each time between woman and man,
Each century unto the other,
Ere time and the ages began.

When drawn is the magical circle,
By sword or athame of power,
Its compass between two worlds lies,
In land of the shades for that hour.

This world has no right then to know it,
And world of beyond will tell naught.
The oldest of Gods are invoked there,
The Great Work of magic is wrought.

For the two are mystical pillars,
That stand at the gate of the shrine,
And two are the powers of nature,
The forms and the forces divine.

The dark and the light in succession,
The opposites each unto each,
Shown forth as a God and a Goddess:
Of this our ancestors teach.

By night he's the wild wind's rider,
The Horn'd One, the Lord of the Shades.
By day he's the King of the Woodland,
The dweller in green forest glades.

She is youthful or old as she pleases,
She sails the torn clouds in her barque,
The bright silver lady of midnight,
The crone who weaves spells in the dark.

The master and mistress of magic,
That dwell in the deeps of the mind,
Immortal and ever-renewing,
With power to free or to bind.

So drink the good wine to the Old Gods,
And Dance and make love in their praise,
Till Elphame's fair land shall receive us
In peace at the end of our days.

And Do What You Will be the challenge,
So be it Love that harms none,
For this is the only commandment.
By Magic of old, be it done!

The next sacred text is the Rede of the Wiccae or the Wiccan Credo. This was written by Lady Gwen Thompson who is said to have recalled this from her grandmother Adriana Porter.

Rede of the Wiccae or Wiccan Credo
By: Lady Gwen Thompson

Bide the Wiccan Laws we must
In Perfect Love and Perfect Trust.

Live and let live,
Fairly take and fairly give.

Cast the Circle thrice about
To keep the evil spirits out.

To bind the spell every time
Let the spell be spake in rhyme.

Soft of eye and light of touch,
Speak but little, listen much.

Deosil go by waxing moon,
Chanting out the Witches' Rune.

Widdershins go by waning moon,
Chanting out the baneful rune.

When the Lady's moon is new,
Kiss thy hand to Her, times two.

When the moon rides at her peak,
Then your heart's desire seek.

Heed the North wind's mighty gale,
Lock the door and drop the sail.

When the wind comes from the South,
Love will kiss thee on the mouth.

When the wind blows from the West,
Departed souls will have no rest.

When the wind blows from the East,
Expect the new and set the feast.

Nine woods in the cauldron go,
Burn them fast and burn them slow.

Elder be the Lady's tree,
Burn it not or cursed you'll be.

When the Wheel begins to turn,

Let the Beltane fires burn.

When the Wheel has turned to Yule,
Light the log, the Horned One rules.

Heed ye Flower, Bush and Tree,
By the Lady, Blessed Be.

Where the rippling waters go,
Cast a stone and truth you'll know.

When ye have a true need,
Hearken not to others' greed.

With a fool no season spend,
Lest ye be counted as his friend.

Merry Meet and Merry Part,
Bright the cheeks and warm the heart.

Mind the Threefold Law you should,
Three times bad and three times good.

When misfortune is enow,
Wear the blue star on thy brow.

True in Love ever be,
Lest thy lover's false to thee.

Eight words the Wiccan Rede fulfill:
As Ye Harm None, Do What Ye Will

Next I will present the Three Fold Law and the Law of Power. The Three Fold Law is a belief and principle by which many Witches live their magickal lives. It explains and relates to how power and energy should and should not be used. It is believed that whatever you send out into the universe, it will come back to you three times the level at which you sent it out. This is why so many Witches take such great care anytime they are practicing their craft; Witches believe that if you do harm, it will come back to you times three.

The Law of Power

1. The power that you are given by the Gods and Goddess should never be used to cause harm or control others. However, should the need arise and you find that you need to protect yourself, your life or the lives of others, then you shall use the power given to you by the Gods and Goddesses to protect those who need protection.
2. You should only use the power given to you by the Gods and Goddesses as the need arises.
3. If you are going to use the power given to you by the Gods and Goddesses for personal gain, then you must see to it that there will be no harm done to anyone else. (There are many that do not believe in using our power for personal gain, but if you think about it, anytime you do a spell to help

someone that is personal gain because you will feel better about yourself for helping, therefore you have used the power for personal gain.)
4. You should not take money as payment for using your power. Doing so can quickly take you over.
5. Using the powers given to you by the Gods and Goddesses for prideful gain will cheapen the mysteries of Wicca, Witchcraft, Paganism and Magick as a whole, therefore it is not wise to use the power for such means.
6. You must always remember that the power given to by the Gods and Goddesses is a sacred gift. Never misuse or abuse the power as it can be taken away from you just as easily as it was given to you.
7. This is the Law of Power.

The next sacred text is the Charge of the God. There are many different versions of this text roaming around in books and on the internet. This is one that I have had in my Book of Shadows and it was handed down to me by the first High Priestess I was ever in a Magickal Circle with. At that time, I had no intentions on writing this book, therefore I honestly have no idea where she got it from. I have searched for the author of this specific version by doing a search of the lines of the text and I have been unable to find an author.

Charge of the God
Listen to the Words of the Horned God,
Who was of old called among men:
Adonis, Tammuz, Dianus, Herne,
Bran, Beli, Lugh, Gwyn,
Dionysus, Osiris, Cernunnos, Pan,
And by many other Names.

O Secret of Secrets,
That art hidden in the being of all that lives,
Not Thee do we adore,
For That which adoreth is also Thou.
Thou art That, and That am I.

I am the Flame that burns in the heart of every being,
And in the core of every Star.
I am Life, and the Giver of Life,
Yet therefore is the Knowledge of Me
The Knowledge of Death and Resurrection.

I am alone, the Lord within ourselves,
Whose Name is Mystery of Mysteries.
I am the Horned God.

I am the Lord of the Universe,
The Father of all living,
The All-Devourer and the All-Begetter.

I am He Whose Seed lies strewn
As glittering Gems across velvet darkness
Within the Womb of the Mother.

I am the Lord of the Shadows
In the darkness of the Underworld,
For I am the Midnight Sun.

I am the Light of the Stars,
And the Spark of the Spirit Eternal,
For I am the God Within.

I am the Horned Leader of the Hosts of Air,
The Leader of the Wild Hunt,
The Judge of Gods and of Men.

I am the Hidden God,
Who ever yet remains,
For I dwell within the secret seed.

I am the seed of grain,
I am the seed of flesh,
I am the Seed of the Stars.

~ 180 ~

I am the Lord of the Heights,
I am the Lord of the Depths,
God of forest, of flock, and of field.

I am the Hunter and Hunted,
I am the wolf and the Shepherd,
I am the vine and the grain.

I am a Guiding Star above you,
I am a bright Flame before you,
I am a smooth Path beneath you.

I am the Light of Life.
I am the Flame of Love.
I am the Horned God!

The final sacred text is the Charge of the Goddess. This text was written by Doreen Valiente and still to this day sends a chill up my spine and brings tears to my eyes when I read it or hear it being read.

Charge of the Goddess
By: Doreen Valiente

Whenever ye have need of anything,
Once in the month and better it be when the moon is full,
Then shall ye assemble in some secret place,
And adore the spirit of me,
Who am Queen of all witches.

There shall ye assemble,
Ye who are fain to learn all sorcery,
Yet have not won its deepest secrets;
To these will I teach all things that are as yet unknown.

And ye shall be free from slavery;
And as a sign that ye be truly free,
You shall be naked in your rites;
And ye shall dance, sing, feast, make music and love,
All in my praise.

For mine is the ecstasy of the spirit,
And mine also is joy on earth;
For my law is love unto all beings.

Keep pure your highest ideals;
Strive ever towards them,
Let nothing stop you or turn you aside.

For mine is the secret door which
Opens upon the Land of Youth,
And mine is the cup of the wine of life,
And the Cauldron of Cerridwen,
Which is the Holy Vessel of Immortality.

~ 182 ~

I am the gracious Goddess,
Who gives the gift of joy unto the heart of man.

Upon earth,
I give the knowledge of the spirit eternal;
And beyond death,
I give peace, and freedom,
And reunion with those who have gone before.

Nor do I demand sacrifice;
For behold, I am the Mother of all living,
And my love is poured out upon the Earth.

I am the beauty of the green earth,
And the white moon among the stars,
And the mystery of the waters,
And the desire of the heart of man.

Call unto thy soul, arise, and come unto me.
For I am the soul of Nature,
Who gives life to the Universe.
From me all things proceed,
And unto me all things must return;
And before my face, beloved of gods and of men,
Let thine innermost divine self be enfolded,
In the rapture of the infinite.

Let my worship be within the heart that rejoicest,
For behold all acts of love and pleasure are my rituals.
Therefore, let there be beauty and strength,
Power and compassion, honor and humility,
Mirth and reverence within you.

And thou who thinketh to seek for me,
Know thy seeking and yearning shall avail thee not,
Unless thou knowest the mystery;
That if that which thou seekest thou findest not within thee,
Thou wilt never find it without thee.

For behold, I have been with thee from the beginning;
And I am that which is attained at the end of desire.

I have left several blank pages here at the end of the book for you to write down any notes that you feel you need to make. Please remember that the information that I have included in this book is not meant to be all inclusive. I want this to be a starting ground for your research into finding more and more ways to practice the Craft without spending a ton of money doing it.

Your journey through the Craft does not have to be an expensive one. I have spent the last seven years looking for ways to make the Craft easier and less expensive. I hope that you will continue to find new ways to make your Magickal journey easier and less expensive.

I wish you the brightest of blessings in your journey!

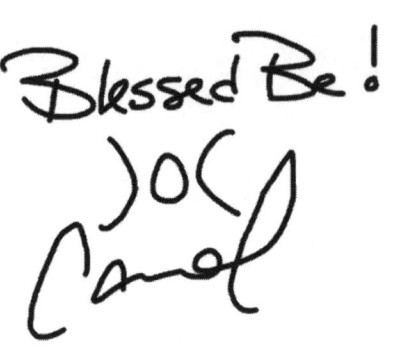

Blessed Be!

)O(

Carol

Printed in Great Britain
by Amazon.co.uk, Ltd.,
Marston Gate.